Georgia

Bed & Breakfast
Cookbook

Recipes from the

Warmth & Hospitality

of Georgia B & Bs

and Historic Inns

By Becky LeJeune

9   8   7   6   5   4   3   2

ISBN 978-1-889593-19-7
PUBLISHED BY:
3D Press
a Big Earth Publishing company
3005 Center Green Drive, Suite 220
Boulder, CO 80301

800-258-5830 (order toll free)
303-443-9687 (fax)
www.bigearthpublishing.com

FRONT COVER PHOTOS
  top: Claremont House; bottom: 1884 Paxton House Inn
BACK COVER PHOTOS
  top: The Beechwood Inn; Middle: Glen-Ella Springs Country Inn;
  bottom: Hamilton-Turner Inn
COVER AND TEXT DESIGN: Rebecca Finkel
EDITING: Becky LeJeune
PRINTED IN China by Imago

The Bed & Breakfast Cookbook Series was originated by Carol Faino & Doreen Hazledine of Peppermint Press in Denver, Colorado in 1996.

Georgia

The Peach State, also known as the Empire State of the South, played a definitive roll in early U.S. history. Georgia's earliest inhabitants left an indelible mark on the land. Mound building cultures such as the Kolomoki, Etowah, and Ocmulgee tribes erected massive earthen mounds throughout the state. Though the tribes had all but disappeared by 1560, these earthen structures still remain today.

In the early 1700s, Georgia was claimed by the British as a way of securing their interests in the new world. The first 113 settlers, led by James Edward Oglethorpe, arrived on February 12, 1733. At first, a royal charter for the land was issued to a philanthropic group who had planned to use the colony as a settlement for the "worthy poor." In 1752, subsidies that supported the colony, however, were not renewed and control was transferred back to the British monarchy.

In 1776, Georgia, along with twelve other colonies, signed the Declaration of Independence, revolting against British rule. In 1788, Georgia became the fourth state to ratify the new United States Constitution. Then, in 1861, Georgia joined the original seven Confederate states and officially seceded from the Union. After years of bloody battles, Georgia was finally admitted back to the Union in 1870.

For years thereafter, the state struggled to rebuild and recover from the effects of the war. The cotton industry boomed making Georgia one of the leading states in the textile industry. Gold was discovered in 1829 resulting in the first U.S. gold rush. Timber and agriculture also became important industries in the state with peaches, pecans, and peanuts as the leading crops. Military training facilities, shipyards, and aircraft plants provided another boom in the economy during WWII. Today, Georgia's rich history, Southern hospitality, delectable cuisine, and amiable climate make it one of the most popular tourist destinations in the South.

STATE SYMBOLS

STATE BIRD: Brown Thrasher

STATE FLOWER: Cherokee Rose

STATE TREE: Live Oak

STATE INSECT: Honeybee

STATE FRUIT: Peach

STATE GEM: Quartz

STATE REPTILE: Gopher Tortoise

STATE VEGETABLE: Vidalia Onion

STATE CROP: Peanut

STATE PREPARED FOOD: Grits

FAMOUS GEORGIANS

Hank Aaron
Paula Deen
Ty Cobb
Alice Walker
Martin Luther King, Jr.
Eli Whitney
President Jimmy Carter
Margaret Miller
Oliver Hardy
Doc Holliday

OTHER STATE FACTS

STATE NICKNAME
Peach State

STATE MOTTO
"Wisdom, Justice, and Moderation"

STATE SONG
Georgia on My Mind

GEOGRAPHICAL FEATURES OF NOTE

HIGHEST POINT: Brasstown Bald 4,784 feet above sea level

Over 250 tree species and 58 protected plants

63 parks, 48 of which are state parks, and 15 historic sites

3 Major River Systems: Chattahoochee, Savannah, and Suwannee; 4 Major Lakes

FUN FACTS ABOUT GEORGIA

- Coca-Cola was invented in Atlanta in 1886 by John Pemberton.

- The first manufactured kazoo, invented by Thaddeus Von Clegg, made its first appearance at the Georgia State Fair in 1852.

- Fast food chain Chick-fil-A is headquartered in, and made its debut in, Atlanta.

- Georgia produces more peanuts than any other state. As a result, the state is sometimes referred to as the Goober State.

Contents

Breads & Muffins

Breads & Muffins

> " The smell of good bread baking,
> like the sound of lightly flowing water,
> is indescribable in its evocation
> of innocence and delight. "
>
> —M. F. K. FISHER

Long Mountain Lodge B&B

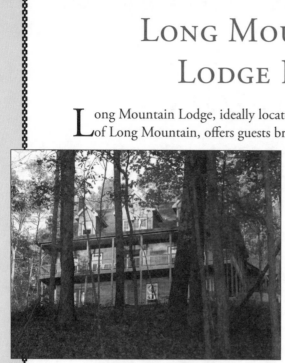

Long Mountain Lodge, ideally located on the southwest slope of Long Mountain, offers guests breathtaking mountain views from each and every one of the inn's guest rooms. In addition to the gorgeous views, and the home away from home feel of the inn itself, each of the guest rooms also features its own wood-burning fireplace and jetted tub, which makes this one romantic mountain retreat!

"I had no idea that such a beautiful place existed in North Georgia. What a perfect complement this lodge is to the quiet and serene mountains. It has rained both nights making this place even more cozy and sleepy. I hiked to the falls and swam in the pool – very cold and refreshing. I also watched some local acts perform last night at the Crimson Moon – highly recommended. Thank you, Dianne, for a delightful stay, and your breakfasts are divine." —GUEST

INNKEEPERS: Dianne & Tim Quigley

ADDRESS: 144 Bull Creek Road, Dahlonega, Georgia 30533

TELEPHONE: (706) 864-2337

E-MAIL: innkeeper@longmountainlodge.com

WEBSITE: www.longmountainlodge.com

ROOMS: 6 Rooms; 5 Suites; 1 Cabin; Private baths

CHILDREN: Children age 16 and older welcome

PETS: Not allowed

Brown Irish Soda Bread

Makes 12 Servings

"While visiting a small pub in the West of Ireland, we enjoyed a moist, somewhat sweet, brown soda bread. I experimented with different ingredients and was able to come up with this recipe, best served warm with butter and marmalade. It has become a favorite amongst our guests, especially when we serve a 'full Irish breakfast.'"

—INNKEEPER, *Long Mountain Lodge Bed & Breakfast*

1½ cups stone-ground wheat flour
½ cup white flour
1 teaspoon salt
2 teaspoons baking soda
1 tablespoon wheat bran
1 tablespoon wheat germ
¼ cup white sugar
¼ cup butter
2 cups buttermilk

Preheat oven to 425°F. In a large bowl, mix together flours, salt, baking soda, wheat bran, and wheat germ. Mix thoroughly. Cut butter into small pieces and rub into flour until dispersed. Make a well in the mixture and pour in the buttermilk, stir but don't over work. Batter should be the texture of thick oatmeal. Pour batter into a greased round cake pan or square glass pan. If desired, sprinkle a little of the wheat bran over the top. Put on a baking tray and bake 10 minutes. Reduce heat to 400°F and bake an additional 20–30 minutes, until a toothpick inserted in the center comes away clean. Remove pan and cool on a wire rack. Once the bread has cooled, remove from pan and wrap in a clean dish towel until ready to serve. Best served warm.

This bread can easily be frozen and reheated.

Jekyll Island Club Hotel

Founded in 1886, the Jekyll Island Club Hotel was once a popular private retreat for some of the country's most prominent families. The inn consists of a collection of cottages that surround the central clubhouse. Acres of lush land and beach ensconce the inn and allow for an intimate setting with a vast array of activities including croquet, bicycle rentals, charter fishing, and golf. The Jekyll Island Hotel features a total of 45 holes – the historic Great

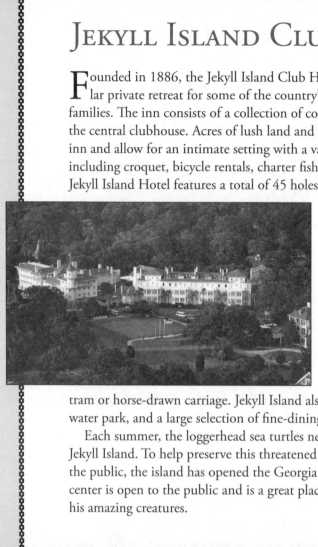

Dunes course and two additional 18-hole layouts.

In addition to the hotel's fabulous list of on-site activities, Jekyll Island itself has quite a bit to offer. You can take a tour of the historic island by either electric tram or horse-drawn carriage. Jekyll Island also has nature tours, a water park, and a large selection of fine-dining restaurants.

Each summer, the loggerhead sea turtles nest on the beaches of Jekyll Island. To help preserve this threatened species and educate the public, the island has opened the Georgia Sea Turtle Center. The center is open to the public and is a great place to learn more about his amazing creatures.

INNKEEPER:	Kevin Runner
ADDRESS:	371 Riverview Drive, Jekyll Island, Georgia 31527
TELEPHONE:	(912) 635-2600; (800) 535-9547
E-MAIL:	mail@jekyllclub.com
WEBSITE:	www.jekyllclub.com
ROOMS:	122 Rooms; 35 Suites: 5 Cottages; Private baths
CHILDREN:	Welcome
PETS:	Not allowed

Vegetable Bread

Makes 2 Dozen Rolls

1 cup milk
⅓ cup sugar
½ cup unsalted butter
½ ounce yeast
1 (1.4 ounce) envelope Knorr Vegetable Soup Mix
1 tablespoon dill weed
1 tablespoon dehydrated onion flakes
23 ounces bread flour
5 ounces egg yolks (approximately 7 yolks)
¼ ounce salt
¼ ounce baking powder

In a mixing bowl, combine milk, sugar, butter, yeast, soup mix, dill, and onion; let stand a few minutes. Add flour, then salt and baking powder and mix with a dough hook. Gradually add the egg yolks as the dough mixes. Allow the bread to knead in the mixer 10–12 minutes. Let dough rest, oiled and covered, in a warm area until it doubles in size.

Preheat oven to 325°F. Portion the dough into rolls of desired size (2–6 ounces each) and round into shape. Let the rolls proof in a warm area until doubled. Slice the tops of the rolls with a sharp knife and bake until nicely browned, about 20 minutes.

North Avenue
Carriage House

More than a bed & breakfast, North Avenue Carriage House offers private accommodations at an affordable price. With space for up to six people, this private guesthouse in historic Ellijay, Georgia is perfect for a family retreat. Exquisite décor featuring period antiques and comfy furniture can be found throughout the house. There is a full kitchen, two bedrooms, a foyer, great room, dining room, and a loft. Breakfast is served on your schedule and features a selection of juices, eggs, bacon, biscuits, muffins, and cereals. The kitchen will also come already stocked with complimentary wine and soft drinks.

If it's just you and your special someone, the North Avenue Carriage House has a special romance package option. Just say

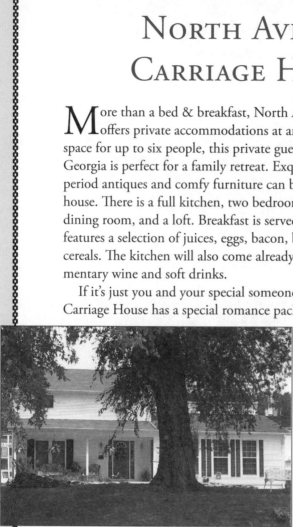

the word and you'll be greeted upon arrival by chilled champagne and a dozen red roses. Enjoy a candle-lit bubble bath in the elegant claw-foot tub and treat yourselves to strawberries and chocolate.

INNKEEPERS: Les & Ouida Leech
ADDRESS: 41 North Avenue, Ellijay, Georgia 30540
TELEPHONE: (706) 889-5658
E-MAIL: oleech@gmail.com
WEBSITE: www.northavenuecarriagehouse.com
ROOMS: 3 Rooms; 2 Suites; 1 Cottage; Private baths
CHILDREN: Children age 6 and older welcome
PETS: Not allowed

Italian Herb Bread

Makes 8 Servings

1¼ cups warm water
1 package Active Dry Yeast
4 tablespoons soft shortening
2 teaspoons salt
2 tablespoons sugar
1½ teaspoons Italian seasoning
½ teaspoon powdered sage
3 cups sifted flour

Pour warm water into a large mixing bowls and sprinkle in yeast; stir until dissolved. Add shortening, salt, sugar, Italian seasoning, sage, and 1½ cups of the flour; beat 2 minutes at medium speed with an electric mixer. Scrape the sides of the bowl frequently. Stir in the remaining flour and beat with a spoon until smooth, about 1½ minutes. Cover dough with a clean cloth and allow to rise in a warm place until double in size, about 30 minutes.

Preheat oven to 375°F. When batter has risen, beat down with 25 strokes. Spread the batter evenly into a greased 9x5-inch loaf pan. Let rise in a warm place until batter has raised ½-inch from the top of the pan, about 40 minutes. Bake 45–50 minutes, or until brown. Remove from pan immediately and brush the top of the loaf with melted butter. Cool and serve with your favorite seasoned olive oil for dipping.

Seventy-Four Ranch B&B

Seventy-Four Ranch Bed & Breakfast is a working ranch dedicated to preserving the skills of the old West and the rich history of the North Georgia Mountains. The ranch sits on land steeped in history. It once belonged to the Cherokee Indians and sits just miles south of where their journey along the Trail of Tears began. Civil War skirmishes occurred in the nearby community, and the inn is said to have been the site of three Moonshine War murders.

In keeping with the tradition and history of the area, each of the inn's guest rooms is decorated with period antiques, artifacts, and original artwork. Guests interested in exploring more of the inn's history are welcome to a self-guided tour of all of the ranch's rooms and buildings.

INNKEEPERS: Larry & Pam Butler

ADDRESS: 9205 Highway 53 West, Jasper, Georgia 30143

TELEPHONE: (706) 692-0123

E-MAIL: reservations@seventyfourranch.com

WEBSITE: www.seventyfourranch.com

ROOMS: 2 Rooms; 1 Suite; 3 Cabins; Private & shared baths

CHILDREN: Welcome

PETS: Welcome; Resident pets

Hearty Zucchini Nut Bread

Makes 1 Loaf

Egg beaters, equivalent to 3 eggs
1 cup sugar
1 cup applesauce, organic recommended
1 cup oil
2 cups grated zucchini
1 teaspoon salt
3 cups flour
3 teaspoons cinnamon
1 teaspoon baking powder
1 teaspoon baking soda
1 teaspoon vanilla extract
1 cup chopped nuts

Preheat oven to 325°F. In a large bowl, mix together eggs, sugar, applesauce, oil, and zucchini. Add dry ingredients and vanilla and mix well to incorporate; fold in nuts. Pour batter into a greased 9x5-inch loaf pan and bake 1 hour.

Allow the bread to cool, then wrap securely and store in the fridge until you are ready to serve. This is an extremely moist and dense bread, if you leave it out it will go crumbly and wet.

THE PRESIDENT'S QUARTERS

Upon arrival at the President's Quarters, each guest is welcomed with coffee, tea, and a selection of cold beverages. Wine and hors d'oeuvres are served each afternoon and features a selection of hot and cold Southern appetizers, finger foods, dips, and cheeses. Each evening, turn down service includes a very special treat – no store bought chocolates for this inn, you'll find a homemade cookie or one of the South's famous pralines waiting on your pillow. And, of course, every stay at the President's Quarters comes complete with a gourmet breakfast.

With its luxury accommodations and amenities, you'll be tempted to never leave! There's still plenty to do and see around Savannah, however, and the inn's convenient location makes them all easily accessible. There are a host of arts and cultural attractions nearby including the City Market, Telfair Museum of Art, and the Savannah Theatre Company. Visit Old Fort Jackson or the nearby Tybee Island Museum and Lighthouse for some historic sightseeing. Eat at one of the many local restaurants like Paula Deen's famous (and casual) The Lady and Sons, and shop the many unique boutiques before returning to the inn for a bit of rest and relaxation.

INNKEEPER: Jane Sales
ADDRESS: 225 East President Street, Savannah, Georgia 31401
TELEPHONE: (912) 233-1600; (800) 233-1776
E-MAIL: info@presidentsquarters.com
WEBSITE: www.presidentsquarters.com
ROOMS: 10 Rooms; 6 Suites; Private baths
CHILDREN: Children age 12 and older welcome
PETS: Not allowed

Cantaloupe Bread

Makes 1 Loaf

*"This is an excellent bread, nice and moist, similar in texture
to pumpkin or zucchini bread. The melon flavor is very delicate,
nearly masked by the spices. Great way to use up extra homegrown
cantaloupe in the summer. Puree and freeze extra in
2 cup containers for use throughout the year."*

—INNKEEPER, *President's Quarters*

3 cups all-purpose flour
1 teaspoon salt
1 teaspoon baking soda
¾ teaspoon baking powder
2 – 2½ teaspoons ground cinnamon
½ teaspoon ground ginger
Pinch of nutmeg
1 cup chopped pecans
3 large eggs
1 cup vegetable oil
2 cups sugar
3 teaspoons vanilla extract
1 cantaloupe

Preheat oven to 325°F. Grease a 9x5-inch loaf pan; set aside. In
a large bowl, combine flour, salt, baking soda, baking powder,
cinnamon, ginger, nutmeg, and pecans; set aside. In another large
mixing bowl, beat the eggs until light and frothy. Add oil, sugar,
and vanilla and mix to combine. Remove the seeds and cut the
rind from the cantaloupe; cut the melon into 2-inch chunks and
purée in a blender or food processor until smooth. Measure 2 cups
of the purée and mix into the egg mixture. Add the flour mixture
to the cantaloupe mixture and stir just to combine – do not overmix. Spoon the batter into the prepared pan and bake 1 hour,
or until a toothpick inserted in the center comes away clean. Let
stand 10 minutes before removing from the pan. Cool on a wire
rack and wrap tightly to store.

HENSON COVE PLACE B&B WITH CABIN

Henson Cove Place Bed & Breakfast is a unique farmhouse-style bed & breakfast located in Hiawassee, Georgia. The peaceful setting brings to mind more laid-back days. Mariah and Dave Nugent spoil their guests by treating them all like they are part of the family. For the utmost in comfortable lodging, excellent food, and gorgeous setting, there is no better place than Henson Cove. The inn features two guest suites with spectacular views. There is also a spacious, and private, self-sufficient cabin located at the back of the property.

Take pleasure in the simpler things in life. The inn's porch swings and rockers allow guests breathtaking pasture and mountain views, and every Southerner can tell you an afternoon on the porch is the best way to allow yourself to unwind, to refresh your body and soul.

INNKEEPERS: Mariah & Dave Nugent

ADDRESS: 1137 Car Miles Road, Hiawassee, Georgia 30546

TELEPHONE: (706) 896-6195; (800) 714-5542

E-MAIL: relax@henson-cove-place.com

WEBSITE: www.henson-cove-place.com

ROOMS: 2 Rooms; 2 Suites; 1 Cabin; Private baths

CHILDREN: Welcome; Call ahead

PETS: Welcome; Resident pet

Strawberry Bread

Makes 2 Loaves

"This recipe was adapted from one found on bbonline.com."

—INNKEEPER, *Henson Cove Place*

1 pound fresh strawberries, quartered

4 eggs

1¼ cups oil

2 cups flour

1¾ cups sugar

3 tablespoons cinnamon

1 teaspoon baking soda

1 teaspoon salt

1 cup chopped walnuts or pecans

Preheat oven to 350°F. Spray 2 9x5-inch loaf pans with non-stick cooking spray. In a large bowl, mix together strawberries, eggs, and oil; add dry ingredients and blend. Divide the mixture evenly between the two loaf pans and bake for 1 hour. Remove from oven and remove loaves from pans. Allow to cool on wire racks or towels.

The Gates House B&B

Gates House B&B opened its doors to guests in 2001 after painstaking and loving renovations. Built in 1873, the home has had a total of four owners over the course of its 130-year history. The home served as a private residence for 63 years before serving as a Knights of Columbus lodge for another six decades. The home

 was then used again as a private residence, with limited guest lodging. Current owners, Tom and Carolyn Gates, purchased the home in 2000 and transformed it into what it is today.

Each of the inn's seven guest rooms has a unique theme with complementing décor. The Green Room, a luxury honeymoon suite, has a grand four-poster bed, working fireplace, and Jacuzzi tub. The elegant Versailles Room features a custom-made king size bed covered in silky gold and cherry colored linens. There is also a second honeymoon suite called the Nest. All of the rooms come with complimentary bath items, private baths, coffee makers, and of course, breakfast is included with every stay.

INNKEEPERS: Tom & Carolyn Gates

ADDRESS: 802 Broadway, Columbus, Georgia 31901

TELEPHONE: (706) 324-6464; (800) 891-3187

E-MAIL: info@gateshouse.com

WEBSITE: www.gateshouse.com

ROOMS: 7 Rooms; 2 Suites; Private baths

CHILDREN: Children age 10 and older welcome

PETS: Not allowed

Banana Nut Bread I

Makes 1 Loaf

1½ cups flour
1 teaspoon baking soda
1 teaspoon baking powder
Pinch of salt
½ cup butter or margarine
2 eggs
1 cup sugar
3 ripe bananas, mashed
¼ cup chopped pecans

Preheat oven to 350°F. In a medium bowl, sift together flour, baking soda, baking powder, and salt; set aside. In a large bowl, mix together butter, eggs, and sugar. Gradually mix dry ingredients and mashed bananas into the sugar mixture and fold in the chopped pecans. Pour the batter into a greased 9x5-inch loaf pan and bake 40–50 minutes, or until a toothpick inserted in the center comes away clean.

This recipe can also be used to make mini or regular sized muffins.

WHITE HOUSE FARM B&B

White House Farm B&B in Montezuma, Georgia, is known for its country comfort and charm and its warm hospitality. Located in the heart of Mennonite country, this working farm and bed and breakfast provides guests the opportunity to escape from the confusion of city life. The home, situated on a 250-acre dairy

farm complete with lush green fields and cropland, was built by innkeepers Crist and Edna Yoder in the 1950s. Per Mennonite tradition, members of the community all chipped in to help build the two-story structure.

Each of the inn's three guest rooms has a unique floral theme with complementing décor. After a wonderful night's sleep on a four-poster bed topped with a handmade quilt, you'll wake to the smell of the freshly baked goods that will accompany your hearty, homemade breakfast. Weather permitting, you have your choice of dining in the open gazebo or the second-story breakfast room. Treat yourself to a relaxing and rejuvenating weekend away from it all and you may never want to leave!

INNKEEPERS: Crist & Edna Yoder

ADDRESS: 1679 Mennonite Church Road, Montezuma, Georgia 31063

TELEPHONE: (478) 472-7942

E-MAIL: home@whitehousefarmbnb.com

WEBSITE: www.whitehousefarmbnb.com

ROOMS: 3 Rooms; Private baths

CHILDREN: Welcome

PETS: Not allowed

Banana Nut Bread II

Makes 10–12 Servings

¾ cup butter
1½ cups sugar
2 eggs
1 teaspoon vanilla extract
1½ cups mashed banana
2 cups flour
¾ teaspoon salt
1 teaspoon baking soda
½ cup buttermilk
1 cup chopped nuts

Preheat oven to 325°F. In a large bowl, cream butter and sugar; add eggs one at a time and mix well to combine. Stir in mashed banana and mix well. In a separate bowl, sift together flour, salt, and baking soda. Add dry ingredients in batches to the banana mixture, alternating with the buttermilk, mixing well between each addition. Fold in chopped nuts. Pour the batter into a greased 9x5-inch loaf pan and bake 1 hour and 15 minutes.

You can also make these as muffins. Simply pour the mixture into greased or lined muffin cups and bake 25–30 minutes (20 minutes for mini-muffins).

COLUMBIA SQUARE INN

Centrally located in the heart of Savannah, Georgia, the Columbia Square Inn offers a peaceful and relaxing atmosphere where you can truly get away from it all without leaving the city. Restaurants, shops, and other Savannah attractions are all just walking distance away.

"Never did I imagine how lovely a time we would have [in Savannah]. From the minute we stepped into Barbara and Royce's home, we were comfortable. Our room overlooking just one of the historic squares was so pretty and had everything we needed to rest, relax, and enjoy our trip. The fridge was filled with fresh fruit, homemade muffins, and assorted beverages. We were free to come and go, and they couldn't have been more helpful to us in finding our way around..."

—Guest

INNKEEPER: Barbara Wall Fricks

ADDRESS: 125 Habersham Street, Savannah, Georgia 31401

TELEPHONE: (912) 236-0444

E-MAIL: N/A

WEBSITE: www.columbiasquareinn.com

ROOMS: 3 Rooms; 1 Suite; Private baths

CHILDREN: Cannot accommodate

PETS: Not allowed

Favorite Poppy Seed Bread

Makes 3 Mini-Loaves

1 package Betty Crocker Butter Pecan cake mix
1 small package Instant Toasted Coconut Pudding
   (Royal brand)
¼ cup poppy seeds
½ cup cooking oil
4 eggs
1 cup hot water

Preheat oven to 325°F. In a large bowl, combine cake mix, pudding mix, poppy seeds, oil, eggs, and hot water; mix until well combined. Pour batter into 3 greased and floured miniature loaf pans. Bake 35 minutes.

Remove from oven and cool 10 minutes before removing loaves from pans.

This bread freezes well. You can slice it straight out of the freezer and spread with cream cheese – it's more like a cake than a bread. Wonderful with strawberry or mandarin cream cheese.

AMERICUS GARDEN INN

B uilt in 1847, the Americus Garden Inn is the oldest house in the area that still sits on its original site. Innkeepers Kim and Susan provide that special personal touch to each guest's stay. Choose from one of the inn's add-on specials and enjoy spa amenities in your own room, a romantic fresh bouquet of flowers to surprise that special someone, or a wine a cheese basket for an afternoon in.

Breakfast at Americus Garden is a true delight. Begin with your choice of six fresh juices, freshly baked breads and muffins, fruit, a hot entrée, and the pancake of the day. With over 40 different varieties of pancake ranging from pumpkin to peanut butter, and apple to sweet potato, you're guaranteed to enjoy this hearty and mouthwatering treat.

INNKEEPERS: Kim & Susan Egelseer

ADDRESS: 504 Rees Park, Americus, Georgia 31709

TELEPHONE: (229) 931-0122; (888) 758-4749

E-MAIL: info@americusgardeninn.com

WEBSITE: www.americusgardeninn.com

ROOMS: 8 Rooms; Private baths

CHILDREN: Children age 10 and older welcome

PETS: Not allowed; Resident pets

Georgia Peach Bread

Makes 2 Loaves

½ cup shortening
1½ cups sugar
2 eggs
2¼ cup puréed peaches
1 teaspoon vanilla extract
2 cups flour
1 teaspoon baking powder
1 teaspoon baking soda
1 teaspoon cinnamon
¼ teaspoon salt
1 cup finely chopped pecans

Preheat oven to 325°F. In a large bowl, cream together shortening and sugar; add eggs and mix thoroughly. Add peach purée, vanilla extract, and dry ingredients to the sugar mixture, mixing until combined. Stir in pecans. Divide the batter between two 5x9-inch greased and floured loaf pans. Bake 55 minutes to 1 hour, until a toothpick inserted in the center comes away clean. Let bread cool for a few minutes before removing from pans.

Pumpkin Corn Muffins

Makes 12 Muffins

1¼ cups flour
1 cup yellow corn meal
⅓ cup granulated sugar
4 teaspoons baking powder
½ teaspoon salt
2 eggs
1¼ cups pure pumpkin
⅓ cup milk
¼ cup vegetable oil

Preheat oven to 375°F and grease 12 muffin cups. In a large bowl, combine flour, cornmeal, sugar, baking powder, and salt. In a medium bowl, beat together eggs, pumpkin, milk, and oil. Add the flour mixture to the egg mixture and mix together thoroughly. Spoon the batter into muffin cups and bake 25–30 minutes, or until a toothpick inserted in the center comes out clean.

Chocolate Ricotta Muffins

Makes 18 Muffins

2⅓ cups flour
1 cup sugar
¾ cup semi-sweet chocolate chips
⅓ cup cocoa
2 teaspoons baking powder
¾ teaspoon salt
1 cup ricotta cheese
1⅓ cups milk
1 teaspoon vanilla extract
¼ cup canola oil
Cooking spray

Preheat oven to 350°F. Spray a ¼-cup muffin tin with non-stick cooking spray, or line with muffin cups. In a large bowl, combine flour, sugar, chocolate chips, cocoa, baking powder, and salt. In a medium bowl, mix together cheese and eggs – add eggs one at a time, beating well after each addition. Whisk in milk and vanilla until well blended. Fold cheese mixture and oil into the flour mixture until just blended. Spoon the batter into muffin cups and bake 25 minutes, or until a toothpick inserted in the center comes out clean. Remove from pan immediately and cool on a wire rack.

CLAREMONT HOUSE

Known for its elegance and hospitality, a stay at the Claremont House is like taking a step back in time. Each of the gorgeous rooms is tastefully appointed with classic Victorian décor. Whether you choose the elegant Elizabeth room, the soothing Magnolia Room, or the romantic Yancey Room, each room features 14-foot ceilings, heart pine wood floors, a fireplace, opulent furnishings, and luxury linens. A gourmet breakfast is included with your stay, and a guest fridge is kept stocked with all sorts of complimentary beverages and snacks.

Just minutes from the Claremont House, you'll find great shops, fine dining, hiking and biking trails, and art exhibits. The staff at the Claremont House is happy to help you plan your dream vacation and is there to assist with your every need, whether it be dinner reservations, show tickets, or recommendations.

INNKEEPERS: Chris & Holly McHagge
ADDRESS: 906 East 2nd Avenue, Rome, Georgia 30161
TELEPHONE: (706) 291-0900; (800) 254-4797
E-MAIL: claremonthouse@comcast.net
WEBSITE: www.theclaremonthouse.net
ROOMS: 4 Rooms; 1 Cottage: Private & shared baths
CHILDREN: Welcome
PETS: Welcome; Resident pets

Blueberry Lemon Muffins

Makes 12 Muffins

*"Local blueberries are available in the summer
to make this great recipe. Stay with us and visit local farms
to pick your own by the gallon!"*

—INNKEEPER, *Claremont House*

2½ cups unbleached, all-purpose flour
¾ cup sugar (white or light brown)
    plus more for sprinkling
1 tablespoon baking powder
⅛ teaspoon fine salt
Freshly grated nutmeg
½ cup (1 stick) unsalted butter
1 cup whole milk
2 large eggs, at room temperature
1 tablespoon finely grated lemon zest
½ teaspoon pure vanilla extract
1½ cup fresh blueberries, rinsed and dried

Preheat oven to 425°F. Line a 12-muffin tin with cupcake liners and set aside. Whisk the flour, sugar, baking powder, salt, and nutmeg together in a medium bowl; set aside. Melt the butter in a microwave-safe bowl, about 30 seconds. Whisk the milk, eggs, lemon zest, and vanilla extract with the butter. Make a small well in the center of the flour mixture. Pour wet ingredients into the well and stir with a wooden spoon until the dry ingredients are moistened but still lumpy. Do not overmix the batter or your muffins will be dense. Gently stir in the blueberries. Divide the batter evenly into the muffin tins and sprinkle the tops generously with additional sugar. Place the muffins into the preheated oven and immediately reduce the temperature to 375°F. Bake about 25 minutes, until muffins are golden brown and a toothpick inserted in the center comes away clean (rotate pan after about 12 minutes to evenly bake).

Cool in the pan on a wire rack for a few minutes before turning muffins out of pan. Allow muffins to continue cooling on rack. Serve warm or at room temperature.

Captain's Quarters B&B

This circa 1902 Classic Renaissance Revival style home was originally a duplex that housed two captains and their families. The home, once a part of the original Army post at Fort Oglethorpe, was bordered at one end by the post's parade ground and the other by the Chickamauga Chattanooga National Battlefield. Fort Oglethorpe was sold by the government to a group of private citizens in 1946,

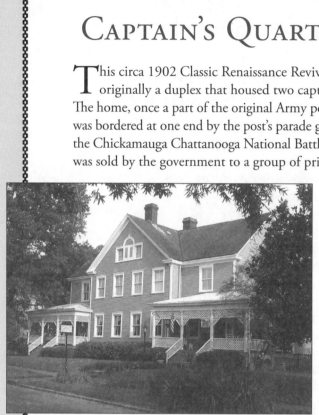

and the town of Ft. Oglethorpe was created. The duplex was opened up in 1988 to create the Captain's Quarter's Bed & Breakfast Inn which is now listed on the Historic National Register.

Tour the historic battleground, enjoy the local cuisine, or drive up to Tennessee's Lookout Mountain, just twenty minutes away. Other nearby activities include white-water rafting, the Tennessee Aquarium, the 6th Calvary Museum, and the Hunter Museum of American Art.

INNKEEPERS: Jim & Julie Powell
ADDRESS: 13 Barnhardt Circle, Fort Oglethorpe, Georgia 30742
TELEPHONE: (706) 858-0624; (800) 710-6816
E-MAIL: info@cqinn.com
WEBSITE: www.cqinn.com
ROOMS: 9 Rooms; 2 suites; Private & shared baths
CHILDREN: Children age 13 and older welcome
PETS: Not allowed; Resident pet

Glazed Pear Muffins

Makes 12 Muffins

"These muffins are often requested by returning guests. The recipe was adapted from one that was featured in Weight Watchers."
—INNKEEPER, *Captain's Quarters Bed & Breakfast*

2 large, ripe Bosc pears, with skin
½ teaspoon cinnamon
⅓ cup sugar
1 teaspoon fresh lemon juice
1 large egg
½ cup sour cream
1 teaspoon vanilla extract
⅓ cup skim milk
2 cups unbleached all-purpose flour
½ teaspoon salt

½ teaspoon baking soda
1 teaspoon baking powder

Glaze:
½ cup powdered sugar
¼ teaspoon ground ginger
¼ teaspoon vanilla extract
3 teaspoons warm water,
  plus more if needed

Preheat oven to 350°F and coat a 12-cup muffin tin with cooking spray. Core the pears and chop into tiny cubes; put in a bowl and add the cinnamon, sugar, and lemon juice. Mix to coat and set aside. In a medium bowl, beat the egg. Whip in the sour cream, 1 teaspoon of the vanilla, and the milk; set aside. In a large bowl, sift together the flour, baking soda, and baking powder. Make a well in the middle of the dry mixture and alternately add the sour cream mixture and the pear mixture. Mix until barely blended – batter will be thick. Divide the batter evenly between the muffin cups and bake 30–35 minutes, or until the muffins are golden brown.

Remove the muffins from the oven and allow them to cool in the pan, for 5 minutes. Meanwhile, combine the glaze ingredients in a small bowl. Swirl some of the glaze over the top of each muffin and smooth with a knife. Place the glazed muffins on a rack over a sheet of aluminum foil (to catch the drips). Serve warm.

JOAN'S ON JONES B&B

This unique three-diamond inn in the heart of historic Savannah began life in 1883 as a Victorian townhouse. Today, Joan's on Jones has been fully restored and offers guests who appreciate the finer things in life a comforting and relaxing lodging experience. Both of the inn's suites have private ground level entrances, period antique furnishings, and can comfortably accommodate up

to four people. The inn is also dog friendly!

New guests will find an array of fresh fruit and a bottle of wine waiting for them in their rooms. Concierge service is available to help you plan your perfect vacation. They'll happily help with dinner recommendations and reservations, they'll also direct you to the best places to find great antiques and shopping, or help to arrange a historic carriage ride through town.

INNKEEPER:	Joan Levy
ADDRESS:	17 West Jones Street, Savannah, Georgia 31401
TELEPHONE:	(912) 234-3863; (888) 989-9806
E-MAIL:	joansonjones@comcast.net
WEBSITE:	http://joansonjones.home.comcast.net
ROOMS:	2 Suites; Private baths
CHILDREN:	Welcome
PETS:	Dogs allowed; Resident pet

Magic Bran Muffins

Makes 12 Jumbo or 24 Regular Muffins

"This is the healthiest muffin and it's yummy, too!"

—INNKEEPER, *Joan's on Jones Bed & Breakfast*

15 ounces raisin bran cereal (about 6 cups)
1 cup raisins
3 cups sugar
3 cups whole-wheat flour
2 cups all-purpose flour
2 teaspoons salt
5 tablespoons baking soda
4 eggs, well beaten
1 quart buttermilk
1 cup canola, or cooking oil

Preheat oven to 400°F. In a large bowl, combine cereal, raisins, and sugar; set aside. In a separate bowl, sift together flours, salt, and baking soda; add to the cereal mixture. In a small bowl, whisk together eggs, buttermilk, and oil. Add the egg mixture to the dry mixture and stir until just moistened. Scoop the batter into the muffin cups, filling them about $2/3$ of the way. Bake 15 minutes.

Muffins will keep in glass containers, refrigerated for up to 2 weeks.

Coffee Cakes, Pound Cakes, Scones, & Biscuits

Coffee Cakes, Pound Cakes, Scones, & Biscuits

Food, like a loving touch
or a glimpse of divine power,
has that ability to comfort.

—NORMAN KOLPAS

Azalea Inn & Gardens

The laid-back charm and easy-going appeal of the South are no more prevalent than here at the Azalea Inn. With a warm and inviting atmosphere, cozy accommodations, and soulful cuisine, Azalea Gardens offers a unique and pleasant stay for anyone who

wants to get away from it all.

This Queen Anne Italianate mansion was originally built in 1889 for Walter K. Coney, a Savannah Civil War blockade-runner. Noted as a romantic garden inn with a lighthearted personality, the Azalea Inn & Gardens has been featured in a number of magazines including *Essence* and *Atlanta Life*. This Savannah historic district bed & breakfast boasts year-round blooming gardens featuring plants native to the southeast as early as the 19th century.

INNKEEPERS: Teresa & Micheal Jacobson
ADDRESS: 217 East Huntingdon Street, Savannah, Georgia 31401
TELEPHONE: (912) 236-2707; (800) 582-3823
E-MAIL: azalea.inn@comcast.net
WEBSITE: www.azaleainn.com
ROOMS: 7 Suites; 2 Cottages; Private & shared baths
CHILDREN: Children age 12 and older welcome
PETS: Not allowed; Resident pets

My Mom's Coffee Cake

Makes 1 Cake

"We traditionally serve this cake only at Thanksgiving and Christmastime. I am not sure how the tradition started, but this cake is so delicious and moist that I think I may have to break tradition!"
—INNKEEPER, *The Azalea Inn*

½ cup shortening
¾ cup granulated sugar
1 teaspoon vanilla extract
3 eggs
2 cups sifted flour
1 teaspoon baking powder
1 teaspoon baking soda
½ pint sour cream (1 cup)
6 tablespoons butter or margarine, softened
1 cup brown sugar, packed
2 teaspoons cinnamon
1 cup chopped nuts

Preheat oven to 350°F. In a medium bowl, cream together shortening, sugar, and vanilla. Add the eggs, one at a time, beating well after each addition. In a separate bowl, sift together the flour, baking powder, and baking soda; add to the creamed mixture alternately with sour cream, blending well after each addition.

Grease a 10-inch tube pan and line the bottom with wax paper. Turn half of the batter into the pan. In a medium bowl, cream softened butter with brown sugar and cinnamon; add the nuts and toss to make crumbly. Place half of the mixture over the first layer of the cake. Spread in the remaining cake batter and top with the last of the nut mixture. Bake 45–50 minutes, or until cake springs back when lightly touched.

Mountain Memories B&B

Perched on a mountaintop in Hiawassee, lies one of Georgia's most romantic inns. With sweeping mountain views from every direction it's easy to see why this inn was chosen as the one of the Most Scenic Views by Bed and Breakfast Journal. Each of the inn's cozy rooms is specially outfitted to provide guests the most comforting and elegant lodging experience ever. These six guest rooms each have their very own private entrances either from the deck or the patio.

Mountain Memories is ideally located just minutes from antique and quilt shops, craft stores, and restaurants. There are also plenty of outdoor activities nearby, including whitewater rafting, hiking, fishing, horseback riding, golf, and boating. Hiawassee even features a Saturday evening concert series in the town square.

INNKEEPERS: Bill & TooToo Cirlot

ADDRESS: 385 Chancey Drive, Hiawassee, Georgia 30546

TELEPHONE: (706) 896-8439; (800) 335-8439

E-MAIL: mtnmem@brmemc.net

WEBSITE: www.mountainmemoriesbandb.com

ROOMS: 6 Rooms; 3 Cabins; Private baths

CHILDREN: Children age 14 and older welcome

PETS: Welcome; Call ahead; Resident pets

Oatmeal Coffee Cake

Makes 1 Cake

1¼ cups boiling water
1 cup oatmeal
2 eggs
½ cup shortening
1 cup brown sugar
1 cup granulated sugar
1½ cups all-purpose flour
1 teaspoon baking soda
1 teaspoon cinnamon
½ teaspoon salt

Topping:
½ cup brown sugar
½ cup granulated sugar
6 tablespoons butter
¼ cup condensed milk
½ teaspoon vanilla extract
1 cup pecans or walnuts

Preheat oven to 350°F and grease a 9x13-inch pan. In a large bowl, mix together boiling water and oatmeal; set aside. In a separate large bowl, cream together shortening and sugars. Add in the eggs and oatmeal and mix to combine. In a medium bowl, sift together flour, baking soda, cinnamon, and salt. Add dry mixture to the oatmeal mixture and combine thoroughly. Pour the batter into the prepared pan and bake 30–35 minutes.

For the topping: While the cake is baking, melt together all of the topping ingredients in a skillet over medium heat. Once the cake is done, spread the topping over the top and place under the broiler just long enough to brown. Watch the cake carefully as the topping can burn quite easily.

Maison LaVigne

Translated, Maison LaVigne means house of vines. Visitors at this quaint b&b are greeted by the lush country garden out front and grapevines climbing the trellis leading to the front walk.

This circa 1906 home has three luxurious guest bedrooms, each named for a different region in France. All three rooms have a unique and romantic décor, but all feature luxury linens from France and Portugal. The inn also has a workout room, sunroom, and tearoom all available to guests.

"Eileen trained at the Ritz Paris and it shows. Her service is a mixture of upscale elegance and down-home hospitality. She knows how to be available every moment of the day without overwhelming. She makes you feel like family but treats you like royalty..." —Guest

INNKEEPER: Eileen Randman

ADDRESS: 3532 South Fulton Avenue, Hapeville, Georgia 30354

TELEPHONE: (404) 766-5561

E-MAIL: atableoffriends@aol.com

WEBSITE: www.maisonlavigne.com

ROOMS: 3 Rooms; Private baths

CHILDREN: Welcome, call ahead

PETS: Welcome; Resident pets

Gâteau du Café

Makes 1 Cake

"The best coffee cake I've ever had."
—INNKEEPER, *Maison LaVigne*

¼ cup unsalted butter, room temp
½ cup sugar in the raw
1 egg, room temp
¾ cup whole milk (a little warm)
1½ teaspoons vanilla extract
1½ cups all-purpose flour
    (King Arthur brand recommended)
1/4 teaspoon sea salt
2 teaspoons baking powder

Topping:
6 tablespoons unsalted butter, must be cold
½ cup flour
½ cup sugar in the raw
Pinch sea salt

Preheat oven to 375°F (400°F for a toaster oven). In a medium bowl, cream together butter and sugar. In a separate bowl, whisk together the egg and milk and add to the butter mixture. Add the vanilla and mix well, scraping down the sides of the bowl so that everything is fully incorporated. In a medium bowl, sift together dry ingredients; add to wet mixture in two parts, making sure that all ingredients are well combined. Pour the batter into a buttered 9-inch cake pan. Scatter the topping over the cake and bake approximately 35 minutes, until a toothpick inserted in the center comes away clean.

For the topping: Place flour and sugar in a medium bowl. Cut in butter and "sand," or crumble together with your fingers, until small pieces are made, but the butter does not melt or warm.

OPEN GATES B&B

Open Gates is a family-run, nature based bed & breakfast located in the charming coastal village of Darien, Georgia. Built in 1876, the home is a great place for nature lovers, history buffs, birders, boating enthusiasts, and anyone else looking to enjoy the peace and

serenity this unique inn has to offer. Innkeepers Kelly and Jeff Spratt purchased the inn in 2000. After loving restorations, the inn welcomed its first guests in 2001 and has been operating ever since.

*"Overlooking the Altamaha River, Open Gates Bed & Breakfast peers graciously at guests through its mossy cloak of giant oaks... Biologists Kelly and Jeff Spratt work to preserve endangered species and do double-duty as innkeepers. They also provide excellent advice on local sights and sounds: Take a ferry to Sapelo Island, one of Georgia's most intriguing barrier islands. Or drive through Harris Neck National Wildlife Refuge and explore – from a safe distance – seven miles of diverse wildlife such as alligators and wood storks. After an all-day outdoor expedition, return to Open Gates for cocktail hour in the library. But don't sleep too late the next morning or you'll miss Kelly and Jeff's superb shrimp and grits." —*COASTAL LIVING

INNKEEPERS: Kelly & Jeff Spratt
ADDRESS: 301 Franklin Street, Darien, Georgia 31305
TELEPHONE: (912) 437-6985
E-MAIL: opengates@earthlink.net
WEBSITE: www.opengatesbnb.com
ROOMS: 5 Rooms; Private & shared baths
CHILDREN: Welcome
PETS: Welcome

Open Gates'
Sour Cream Coffee Cake

Makes 1 Cake

2 sticks butter, softened
2 cups sugar
2 eggs
1 teaspoon vanilla extract
2 cups all-purpose flour
1 teaspoon salt
1 tablespoon baking powder
1 cup sour cream

Nut Mixture:
1 cup chopped walnuts
1 cup brown sugar
1 tablespoon cinnamon

Preheat oven to 350°F and grease one bundt pan. In a large bowl, beat together the butter and sugar with an electric mixer until the mixture is fluffy. Add the eggs and the vanilla and beat on high speed for 1 minute. Mix in flour, salt, and baking powder until fully combined. Add the sour cream and beat the mixture until smooth.

In a small bowl combine all of the ingredients for the nut mixture and sprinkle about ⅓ into the bottom of the greased bundt pan. Spoon in half of the cake batter and top with another ⅓ of the nut mixture. Top with the remaining cake batter and sprinkle the rest of the nut mixture over the top. Bake for 1 hour.

HOLLY COURT INN

Historic Holly Court Inn is actually two combined "plain-style" Federal period homes, each dating from the 1830s. The inn sits on two gorgeous landscaped acres just two blocks from Washington town square. The inn features two elegant guest rooms and two luxury suites. Stately antiques and period furniture can

be found throughout the home, lending an authentic old South feel to the entire inn.

Your day at the Holly Court Inn begins with a mouthwatering Southern breakfast. After that you can stroll into town and enjoy the sites. Antebellum homes and traditional architecture grace the town's streets. There are two historic landmarks and four national register districts all within city limits. The town square offers a variety of quaint shops and fine dining. When you return to the inn, an afternoon sherry will be waiting for you in the parlor. In the evening, you can arrange a candlelight dinner at the inn for you and that special someone.

INNKEEPERS: Phil & Margaret Rothman
ADDRESS: 301 South Alexander Avenue, Washington, Georgia 30673
TELEPHONE: (706) 678-3982; (866) 456-5928
E-MAIL: info@hollycourtinn.com
WEBSITE: www.hollycourtinn.com
ROOMS: 4 Rooms; 2 Suites; Private baths
CHILDREN: Welcome
PETS: Not allowed; Resident pets

Raspberry-Almond Coffee Cake

Makes 8 Servings

"This recipe was adapted from the Joy of Cooking:
All About Breakfast & Brunch *cookbook."*
—INNKEEPER, *Holly Court Inn*

Dry breadcrumbs
2 cups all-purpose flour
1⅛ cups sugar
1 teaspoon salt
1¼ cups (10 tablespoons)
   unsalted butter
1 teaspoon baking powder
½ teaspoon baking soda
¾ cup buttermilk or yogurt
1 large egg

1 teaspoon vanilla extract
1 teaspoon almond extract
½ cup seedless raspberry jam

Topping:
¾ cup ground almonds
½ cup sugar
1 large egg yolk
1 teaspoon almond extract

Preheat oven to 350°F. Grease the bottom and sides of a 9-inch springform pan. Sprinkle dry breadcrumbs into the bottom of the pan. In a large bowl, mix together flour, sugar, and salt. Add the butter and mix until the mixture resembles coarse crumbs – a food processor works well for this. Remove 1 cup of the mixture and reserve for topping. To the large bowl, add baking powder and baking soda; add buttermilk or yogurt, egg, vanilla, and almond extract and mix until the mixture is smooth and fluffy. Pour batter into the prepared pan and smooth the top. Stir raspberry jam until it is fluid and spread over the batter.

For the topping: Add the ground almonds, sugar, egg yolk, and almond extract to the reserved 1 cup of crumb mixture. Mix well with fingers and sprinkle evenly over the cake. Bake 50–65 minutes, until a toothpick inserted in the center comes away clean. Cool in pan on a rack for 10 minutes. Slide a thin knife around the sides of the pan and remove. Cool on rack an additional 1½ hours before serving.

WHITAKER-HUNTINGDON INN

After painstaking renovations, Bill and Debbie Saxman have managed to preserve the genteel historic setting of this 1883 Italianate home while providing guests a truly Southern vacation experience they will never forget. The Whitaker-Huntingdon Inn is  filled with period antiques including items acquired from the estates of previous owners. This effort has paid off as a stay at the Whitaker-Huntingdon really does feel like a step back in time.

Today, the inn features two luxury guest suites comprised of one bedroom with queen sized bed, a sitting room with a queen-sized fold-out, private bath, and full kitchenette stocked with all sorts of breakfast fixings. Plans once included breaking the rooms up into five separate guest rooms. To preserve the character and design of the home, Bill and Debbie elected not to change the layout. The result is a more intimate vacation experience that allows guests to enjoy the grand living experience of the past while still taking advantage of today's modern conveniences.

INNKEEPERS: Bill & Debbie Saxman

ADDRESS: 6002 Whitaker Street, Savannah, Georgia 31401

TELEPHONE: (912) 232-8911; (877) 232-8911

E-MAIL: whinn@aol.com

WEBSITE: www.whinn.com

ROOMS: 4 Rooms; 2 Suites; Private baths

CHILDREN: Welcome

PETS: Not allowed; Resident pets

Granny's Lemon Pound Cake

Makes 1 Cake

1 (8-ounce) package cream cheese, softened
4 eggs
1 (1 pound 2 ounce) package yellow cake mix
¾ cup milk (whole or 2%)
2 tablespoons grated lemon peel

Preheat oven to 350°F. Grease and flour a 9-inch tube pan (or two small loaf pans). In a large bowl, using an electric mixer set at medium speed beat the cream cheese until fluffy. Scrape the beaters then add eggs, one at a time, beating well. Lower speed to low and add cake mix in three batches; beat until well combined. Blend in lemon peel.

Pour batter into prepared pan(s) and bake 55 minutes, or until top begins to brown.

Let cake cool 15 minutes. Dust with confectioners' sugar if desired.

PURA VIDA USA

Pura Vida USA is where vacationers go to rejuvenate their souls. This wellness and yoga retreat, located in gorgeous Dahlonega, Georgia, is designed to give you maximum rest and relaxation in a serene environment. Between the reproduction 1920s farmhouse, the barn house, cabins, and the cottages, the inn has a total of 24 guest rooms to choose from. With your stay, you can choose from a host of different packages. Some of the amenities/activities offered include healthy meals, daily yoga sessions, spa treatments, nature and winery tours.

"My husband and I stayed at Pura Vida USA for our 1st year anniversary. We opted for a two-night package with meals, complimentary yoga classes, and two spa treatments. If you enjoy wine, pampering, and an escape from your laptop and TV, then this is the place for you. We stayed in the Farmhouse, which was very comfortable… At night, we enjoyed the huge outdoor Jacuzzi tub. I'm hoping that we will return to Pura Vida for our 2nd anniversary." —GUEST

INNKEEPER: Beckie Fairley
ADDRESS: 400 Blueberry Hill, Dahlonega, Georgia 30533
TELEPHONE: (706) 865-7678; (866) 345-4900
E-MAIL: reservations@puravidausa.com
WEBSITE: www.puravidausa.com
ROOMS: 24 Rooms; 1 Suite; 8 Cabins; Private baths
CHILDREN: Welcome
PETS: Small pets welcome

Blueberry Pound Cake

Makes 1 Cake

1 stick butter
⅓ cup oil
1½ cups sugar
3 eggs
1 cup plain flour
½ cup milk
1 teaspoon vanilla flavoring
1 cup fresh blueberries*

Blueberry Glaze:
1 cup powdered sugar
¼ cup drained blueberries, crushed

Preheat oven to 325°F. In a large bowl, cream together butter, oil, and sugar. Add the eggs and flour alternately, continuing to mix and combine. Add milk and vanilla and blend well with a mixer. Fold in blueberries with a spatula (not with a mixer) and pour the batter into one greased and floured bundt pan. Bake about 1 hour, or until a toothpick inserted in the center comes away clean. Remove from oven and drizzle with blueberry glaze.

For the glaze: Stir ingredients together using a spatula. If the mixture is too stiff, add a few drops of milk.

*If using frozen blueberries, thaw completely then rinse and drain. You want no liquid in the blueberries.

THE ZEIGLER HOUSE INN

Located in the heart of Savannah's National Landmark Historic District is the luxurious and romantic Zeigler House Inn. Originally built in 1856, this Italianate style home has been lovingly restored to its pre-Civil War splendor. With its heart pine floors, elegant ceiling medallions, slate and wood fireplaces, and dramatic staircase, guests will feel as though they have stepped into something straight out of *Gone With the Wind* – with modern amenities, of course.

Zeigler house is conveniently located just minutes from downtown Savannah. Innkeeper Jackie Heinz will gladly help you arrange a tour, make a reservation at one of River Street's wonderful restaurants, and make suggestions for other "special events" to ensure that your stay in Savannah is perfect.

INNKEEPER: Jackie Heinz

ADDRESS: 121 West Jones Street, Savannah, Georgia 31401

TELEPHONE: (912) 233-5307

E-MAIL: innkeeper@zeiglerhouseinn.com

WEBSITE: www.zeiglerhouseinn.com

ROOMS: 3 Rooms; 2 Suites; Private baths

CHILDREN: Call ahead

PETS: Not allowed; Resident pets

Zeigler House Scones

Makes 6 Scones

"This recipe has been developed over the last 2 years, it is now a guest favorite. This is not a dry or hard scone recipe. It is very light, moist, and full of flavor. Most guests comment that they didn't think they liked scones until they tried these."
—INNKEEPER, *The Zeigler House Inn*

2 cups all-purpose flour
¼ cup sugar
1 teaspoon salt
1 tablespoon baking powder
5 tablespoons sweet, unsalted butter, cubed
1 cup heavy cream
½–¾ cup dried fruit of choice*
1 egg
2 tablespoons water

Preheat oven to 400°F. In the bowl of a food processor add the first four dry ingredients and pulse to mix. Add butter and process until the mixture looks like coarse meal. Add fruit or other add-ins and turn on the processor; add cream in a steady stream until the dough comes together. Turn the dough out onto a floured surface and knead a few times to bring together. Divide the dough into 6 equal balls and place on a cookie sheet lined with parchment paper. In a small bowl, whisk together the egg and water; brush the mixture over the tops of scones and sprinkle with sugar. Bake 20 minutes, remove from oven and cool on wire racks.

*Optional add-ins: nuts, chocolate chips, 1 teaspoon vanilla extract, 2 teaspoons cinnamon, orange or lemon zest, cheese, bacon bits. Some of our favorite combinations for these scones are Orange Cranberry, Cinnamon Raisin, White Chocolate Cherry, Cherry Almond, Lemon Blueberry, Bacon Cheddar, Mixed Berry, and Blueberry.

1890 King-Keith House

Built in 1890, the King-Keith house is one of Atlanta's premier historic bed & breakfasts. Architect and owner Windell Keith and his wife Janet have lovingly and painstakingly restored the romantic historic home to its original splendor. This Queen-Anne style home is now proud to be one of the most photographed homes in all of Atlanta!

Elegant twelve-foot ceilings, carved fireplaces and period antiques grace this magnificent inn, treating guests to a taste of authentic historic Atlanta. Begin each day with a full homemade breakfast in the inn's elegant dining room, and enjoy complimentary snacks and beverages in the inn's private garden each evening before retiring.

INNKEEPERS:	Windell & Janet Keith
ADDRESS:	889 Edgewood Avenue, NE, Atlanta, Georgia 30307
TELEPHONE:	(404) 688-7330; (800) 728-3879
E-MAIL:	kingkeith@mindspring.com
WEBSITE:	www.kingkeith.com
ROOMS:	5 Rooms; 1 Suite; 1 Cottage; Private & shared baths
CHILDREN:	Welcome
PETS:	Not allowed

Currant Buttermilk Scones

Makes 6 Scones

3 cups all-purpose flour
½ cup sugar
2½ teaspoons baking powder
6 ounces unsalted butter, chilled
    and cut into small pieces
1 cup currants
1 cup buttermilk
Zest of 1 large orange
2 tablespoons half & half or buttermilk

Preheat oven to 400°F. In the bowl of a food processor, mix the flour, sugar, baking powder, and baking soda. Add the butter and combine, pulsing on and off until the mixture resembles coarse meal. Transfer the mixture to a large bowl and add the currants, buttermilk, and orange zest. Mix with a fork until just blended. Turn the dough out onto a floured surface and knead 8-10 times. Shape the dough into a 10-inch circle, about ¾-inch thick, and cut into diamond wedges. Place the scones on a greased cookie sheet and brush tops with cream. Bake 15–20 minutes.

Variation: Use white chocolate chips and chopped, dried apricot in lieu of the orange and currants.

THE PRESIDENT'S QUARTERS

The exclusive President's Quarters in Savannah, Georgia, is actually two historic Federal mansions. Each of the inn's 15 spacious guest rooms features luxury amenities and accommodations including gas fireplaces, plush linens, and elegant furnishings. Two of the inn's suites have their own private entrances, and four of the rooms have their own private balconies. Then there are the loft rooms. Loft suites include their own living/dining areas, wet bar, and an extra half-bath, great for vacationers looking for a more elegant but homey feel. Each room is named to honor one of the U.S. presidents who visited the Southern city.

"We wanted to stay in the historic district in beautiful Savannah, and experience true Southern hospitality…Having been raised in the South, I certainly know what this hospitality means and the President's Quarters did not let us down. The staff was so friendly, respectful, and helpful. . .The breakfast was exceptional, with choices that were varied enough that we truly got what we wanted, and it was plentiful enough that we still were not hungry come lunch time…we will be back to Savannah for nothing more than to stay with our new friends at this lovely bed and breakfast." —GUEST

INNKEEPER:	Jane Sales
ADDRESS:	225 East President Street, Savannah, Georgia 31401
TELEPHONE:	(912) 233-1600; (800) 233-1776
E-MAIL:	info@presidentsquarters.com
WEBSITE:	www.presidentsquarters.com
ROOMS:	10 Rooms; 6 Suites; Private baths
CHILDREN:	Children age 12 and older welcome
PETS:	Not allowed

Mr. Green's PQ Signature Bacon & Cheese Scones

Makes 12 Scones

"Supposedly, these are the scones that are served at the palace. We modified the recipe by increasing the butter and adding the bacon. Dill is good addition to these scones as well."
— INNKEEPER, *President's Quarters*

¾ cup butter
3½ cups flour
Pinch of salt
1 tablespoon baking powder
½ cup sugar
1 egg
½ cup milk
¼ cup shredded cheese
6–8 slices cooked bacon, cut up

Preheat oven to 350°F. In a large bowl, cut together the butter, flour, salt, and baking powder; dough will be coarse. Add the sugar. Make a well in the center of the dough; add the egg and a small amount of milk and blend to a nice, smooth dough. If the mixture is dry, add more milk as needed. Fold in the cheese and the bacon.

Place the dough on a flat, floured surface and roll out until dough is ½-inch thick. Cut the scones using a cutter with a 2-inch fluted edge. Place the scones on a lightly greased baking sheet and brush the tops with 1 beaten egg. Bake 10–15 minutes. Remove from oven and allow to cool before serving.

THE FARMHOUSE INN

Just minutes from historic Madison, Georgia, travelers will find the charming Farmhouse Inn. With its five private guestrooms, two-bedroom cottage, and four-bedroom farmhouse, all uniquely appointed with quaint and cozy décor, guests are sure to feel both welcome and relaxed in this quiet country setting. This is the ideal vacation spot for a romantic weekend getaway, or even a family vacation. The inn and its expansive grounds offer guests plenty to while away the time – wooded trails, fishing ponds, and creek-side gulleys are perfect for nature lovers. The inn also offers guests the use of birding baskets complete with binoculars and birdcalls for birding enthusiasts. You can also pack a picnic to take out to nearby Riverside Landing, perfect for a lazy afternoon in the sun.

"A country sanctuary.... Guests rediscover the simple pleasures of life at the Farmhouse Inn."
—SOUTHERN LIVING MAGAZINE

INNKEEPER: Melinda Hartney
ADDRESS: 1051 Meadow Lane, Madison, Georgia 30650
TELEPHONE: (706) 342-7933; (866) 253-0023
E-MAIL: innkeeper@thefarmhouseinn.com
WEBSITE: www.thefarmhouseinn.com
ROOMS: 2 Rooms; 3 Suites; 2 Cottages; Private baths
CHILDREN: Welcome
PETS: Not allowed; Resident pets

Rosemary Biscuits

Makes 12 Small Biscuits

"Rosemary is the herb for remembrance. We use it as a theme around here for guests to remember their experience with us. As a thank you gift, guests receive a bar of homemade rosemary soap with a sprig of fresh rosemary from our garden."
—INNKEEPER, *Farmhouse Inn*

2 cups self-rising flour
1 stick real butter
8 ounces sour cream
Fresh rosemary

Preheat oven to 350°F and spray the cups of a mini-muffin tin with non-stick cooking spray. Combine the flour, butter, and sour cream in a medium bowl. Mix until fully combined, but be careful not to overmix. Roll a spoon-sized amount of the dough into a ball in your hand. If the dough is too sticky, roll in some additional flour. Roll the ball in the rosemary until 6–10 pieces stick to the exterior of the dough. Place the dough into one cup of a mini-muffin tin and repeat until each cup is filled with one dough ball.

Bake 12–14 minutes, until biscuits are slightly brown. Remove from oven and allow to sit 5 minutes before removing from pan.

THE WINDOWS INN B&B

The Windows Inn Bed & Breakfast was originally built as a private home in 1913. Although the home has since been fully renovated and completely updated, it still retains its original grace and splendor - hard wood floors, high ceilings, period furnishings,

and original fixtures can still be found throughout the inn. The inn's large open porch and comfy chairs provide a welcome afternoon retreat, and the peaceful gardens are a great place for a quiet evening walk.

Each of the inn's four guest rooms has a different floral theme and has been decorated with historic antiques. A full Southern breakfast is served each morning and features items ranging from the inn's signature Southern Touch Quiche to Puffed French Toast and the Baked Breakfast Casserole.

INNKEEPERS: Lyle & Janis Lewis

ADDRESS: 206 South 4th Avenue, McRae, Georgia 31055

TELEPHONE: (229) 868-2067

E-MAIL: jklewis1@windstream.net

WEBSITE: www.thewindowsinn.com

ROOMS: 4 Rooms; Private & shared baths

CHILDREN: Children age 12 and older welcome

PETS: Not allowed

Stuffed Angel Biscuits

Makes 12–18 Servings

"I took this recipe and put my own spin on it by patting down the dough… and stuffing it with a ham and Swiss mixture. I can the biscuit mixture up ahead of time, use as much as I want each day…, and refrigerate the rest. It lasts up to a week in the refrigerator."
—INNKEEPER, *The Windows Inn Bed & Breakfast*

5 cups all-purpose flour
¼ cup sugar
1 teaspoon baking powder
1 teaspoon salt
1 cup shortening
1 package yeast
¼ cup warm water
2 cups buttermilk
Ham and Swiss cheese,
    chopped together in the food processor

In a large bowl, mix together the flour, sugar, baking powder, and salt. Cut in the shortening and make a well in the center of the mixture. In a small bowl, dissolve the yeast in the water; stir into the dry mixture with the buttermilk, stirring until the mixture forms a ball. Refrigerate in a covered bowl for up to a week.

When you are ready to use the dough, preheat your oven to 400°F. Roll the dough out on a lightly floured surface and cut out the biscuits. Pat each one into a circle making the dough as thin as you can. Place spoonfuls of the ham and Swiss mixture onto the center of each biscuit and fold over to seal. Place biscuits on a lightly greased cookie sheet and brush each one with a bit of melted butter. Bake 20–23 minutes until golden brown. Brush with additional melted butter before serving.

Joan's on Jones B&B

Joan's on Jones is an elegant Victorian town-home with two separate guest suites, each with their own private, ground level access. Upon entering the Jones Street Suite, guests will find a tastefully appointed front parlor that opens up to the bedroom and its elegant

four-poster rice bed. The room has its own refrigerator and icemaker, fresh fruit, wine, and breakfast fixings.

The Garden Suite, accessible through the inn's secluded walled garden, is another oasis in the heart of the city. The sound of the garden's fountain will follow you as you enter the front sitting room. The bedroom was once a kitchen and still boasts its original fireplace. In addition to the same amenities found in the Jones Street Suite, the Garden Suite also has its own full kitchen and a patio in the garden. For larger parties, the two suites can be opened up to accommodate up to seven guests.

INNKEEPER: Joan Levy

ADDRESS: 17 West Jones Street, Savannah, Georgia 31401

TELEPHONE: (912) 234-3863; (888) 989-9806

E-MAIL: joansonjones@comcast.net

WEBSITE: http://joansonjones.home.comcast.net

ROOMS: 2 Suites; Private baths

CHILDREN: Welcome

PETS: Dogs allowed; Resident pet

Southern Cheese Biscuits

Makes 6–8 Biscuits

2 cups all-purpose flour
1 teaspoon salt
½ teaspoon baking soda
½ cup shortening
¾ cup shredded sharp cheddar cheese
½ cup buttermilk
Pinch cayenne pepper
Melted butter to brush on top

Preheat oven to 500°F. In a medium bowl, mix together the flour, salt, and baking soda. Using a pastry blender cut in the shortening and cheese, mixing until the batter forms soft crumbs. Make a well in the center of the batter and add the buttermilk. Quickly fold in the buttermilk, using your hands. Turn the dough out onto a floured surface and fold dough over on itself 3–4 times. Roll the dough out until it is about ¾-inch thick. Cut with a 3-inch biscuit cutter and brush tops with butter. Bake 5 minutes and then lower oven temperature to 400°F and bake an additional 5 minutes.

THE DODGE HILL INN

A stay at The Dodge Hill Inn has been described by some guests as being "like coming home to Mother, but without the guilt!" This circa 1912 home is the only bed & breakfast in Eastman, Georgia. Innkeepers Ann, Don, and Helen offer guests their rooms, their ears, and their hearts as well as their fine southern hospitality and hearty homemade cuisine.

Whether you are looking for a charming southern vacation, a relaxing and private getaway, or a romantic trip for two, the Dodge Hill Inn is the perfect place for you.

INNKEEPERS: Ann & Don Dobbs & Helen Peterson
ADDRESS: 5021 Ninth Avenue, Eastman, Georgia 31023
TELEPHONE: (478) 374-2644
E-MAIL: missann@dodgehillinn.com
WEBSITE: www.dodgehillinn.com
ROOMS: 2 Rooms; 2 Suites; 3 Cottages; Private baths
CHILDREN: Welcome
PETS: Not allowed

Buttermilk Biscuits

Makes 8-12 Servings

"We learned biscuit making from our mothers! This recipe can also be found in our own cookbook A Gracious Plenty available at the inn. Helen always makes biscuits and they are always delicious, high, puffy, and soft. If you wish to make them ahead bake them to light brown, cover and reheat when ready to serve..."
—INNKEEPER, *Dodge Hill Inn Bed & Breakfast*

2 cups sifted, self-rising flour
4–5 tablespoons Crisco
¾ cup sweet milk or
   ⁴/₅ cup buttermilk

Cinnamon variety:
⅓ cup butter
⅓ cup granulated sugar
1 teaspoon cinnamon
1 cup powdered sugar
2 tablespoons half & half
1 tablespoon vanilla

For regular biscuits: Preheat oven to 450°F. Sift the flour, measure and sift again into a mixing bowl. Cut in the shortening using a pastry blender, working from the outside of the bowl toward the center and turning the bowl as you work. Add the milk – you may need to add just a bit more if the batter is too dry. Flour hands well, lift the dough and place it on a pastry cloth. Add more flour if necessary. Knead the dough a few turns, lifting it with the fingers and pushing it forward with the heel of the hand. Roll dough out on a floured surface to about ¼-inch thickness. Cut using a biscuit cutter and place biscuits on a baking sheet. Bake about 8 minutes, until biscuits are done.

For cinnamon biscuits: Preheat oven to 425°F. Mix as above and roll dough into a rectangle. Melt butter and spread over dough. In a small bowl, combine the granulated sugar and cinnamon; sprinkle mixture over dough. Roll dough, long side of the rectangle up to make a roll. Cut to make biscuits of desired thickness – about ½-inch each. Place on a cookie sheet and bake 8 minutes, until done. Beat remaining ingredients together using a hand mixer – mixture should be creamy. Spread over hot cinnamon biscuits to serve.

WISTERIA HALL

Wisteria Hall in historic Waynesboro, Georgia, derives its name from the magnificent 8-foot tall stained glass window overlooking the grand, central staircase. This neoclassical Greek revival mansion, built in 1900, stands four stories tall and is the tallest surviving residence of the era.

Each of the four luxurious guest rooms features its own different theme. Vintage quilts, antique furnishing, oak beds, and period décor can be found in each of the spacious rooms. Guests will delight in the little extras that can be found throughout the inn as well. For example, the Liberty Room has a display of antique dolls and the Hopkins Room has a massive four-poster, canopied bed. Common areas in the inn include two separate parlors, sunroom, balcony room, and a veranda. Breakfast is served each morning in the formal dining room.

INNKEEPERS: Ralph & Nancy Lynn
ADDRESS: 824 Myrick Street, Waynesboro, Georgia 30830
TELEPHONE: (706) 437-1323
E-MAIL: wisteriahall@comcast.net
WEBSITE: www.wisteriahallonline.com
ROOMS: 4 Rooms; Private baths
CHILDREN: Children age 10 and older welcome
PETS: Not allowed

Pecan Cinnamon Rolls

Makes 10 Servings

*"People will think you spent hours cooking these rolls,
but they are very simple and taste fantastic!"*
—INNKEEPER, *Wisteria Hall, Waynesboro*

1 can Pillsbury Flaky Biscuits
¼ cup melted butter
½ cup chopped nuts
1 teaspoon cinnamon
1 cup brown sugar

Icing:
1 cup powdered sugar
Flavored Coffee Mate (of choice)

Preheat oven to 350°F. Separate each biscuit into 2–3 pieces –
to make layered rolls. Lightly spray a muffin tin with non-stick
cooking spray and place one biscuit piece into each cup. In a
small bowl, mix together the nuts, cinnamon, and brown sugar.
Brush the top of each biscuit with melted butter and with the
nut mixture. Top with the second biscuit piece and repeat. Top
with final biscuit piece and brush with butter. Bake 30 minutes.
Remove rolls from the muffin tin and top with icing to serve.

For the icing: Mix the powdered sugar with enough Coffee Mate
to make an icing of desired consistency. Drizzle over rolls.

French Toast, Pancakes, & Waffles

French Toast, Pancakes, & Waffles

> *...the joy of living*
> *was wrapped up*
> *in the delights of food.*
>
> —LAURA ESQUIVAL

Ashford Manor
Bed & Breakfast

Guests at Ashford Manor Bed & Breakfast will experience the privacy and privileges of a graceful residence without giving up the luxuries of a first-class hotel. In each of the six elegant guest rooms, travelers will find luxurious robes and bath products, an in-room refrigerator, and a coffeemaker stocked with private-label teas and coffees. Each uniquely appointed room is decorated with an eclectic selection of items found on the proprietors' various travel excursions.

Attention to detail is very important at the Ashford Manor and Mario, Jim, and Dave want to make sure that each and every guest will remember their stay at the inn as being a relaxing and rejuvenating one.

INNKEEPERS: Mario Castro, Jim & Dave Shearon

ADDRESS: 5 Harden Hill Road, Watkinsville, Georgia 30677

TELEPHONE: (706) 769-2633

E-MAIL: ashfordmanor@charter.net

WEBSITE: www.ambedandbreakfast.com

ROOMS: 5 Rooms, 1 Suite; Private baths

CHILDREN: Children age 14 and older welcome

PETS: Dogs allowed

Ashford Manor Crème Brûlée French Toast

Makes 4 Servings

"We took several of our favorite French toast recipes and combined them into this very unique, very Ashford Manor recipe. Plan ahead, this dish will need to be prepared at least 8 hours ahead of time."

—INNKEEPER, *Ashford Manor*

1 stick (8 tablespoons) unsalted butter
1 cup packed brown sugar
2 tablespoons corn syrup
Grated peel of 1 orange
1 (8-9 inch) round country-style bread,
    Challah, baguette, or Hawaiian Bread
1 (8-ounce) package cream cheese
6 large eggs
2 cups half & half
1 teaspoon vanilla extract
1 teaspoon Grand Marnier or Triple Sec
1 teaspoon salt

Melt together the butter, brown sugar, and corn syrup in a small heavy saucepan over moderate heat; stir until smooth. Pour into a 13x9-inch baking dish and sprinkle with grated orange peel. Cut the bread into ¾-inch thick slices. Arrange the bread in one layer over the top of the sugar mixture, squeezing slightly so that they all fit. Cut the cream cheese into ¼-inch cubes and flatten with your fingertips to cover the bread layer. In a medium bowl, whisk together the eggs, half & half, vanilla, Triple Sec, and salt and pour evenly over bread. Refrigerate, covered, for at least 8 hours (can be refrigerated up to 24 hours).

Place an oven rack in the center of the oven and preheat to 350°F. Bake French toast, uncovered, until toast is puffed and edges are pale golden – 35–40 minutes. With a spatula, flip over the French toast so that they are served syrup side up. Use a brûlée torch to put the final crystallized touch to the topping.

The Hearthstone Lodge

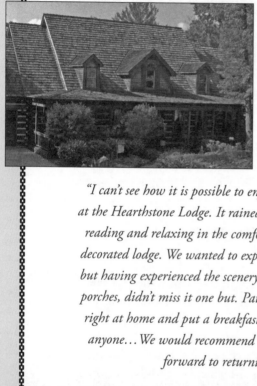

Situated in the lush Georgia mountains, between Fort Mountain State Park and Carters Lake, is the rustic and secluded Hearthstone Lodge. This serene mountain getaway offers nature lovers and vacationers a private and romantic vacation experience like no other. Guests are invited to enjoy the wonderful nature surrounding the inn – a short hike will take you to a magnificent 50-foot waterfall, the perfect place for a private afternoon picnic. Nature trails will also take you to the top of the summit where you'll enjoy a breathtaking view of the Chattahoochee National Forest.

"I can't see how it is possible to enjoy a b&b any more than we did at the Hearthstone Lodge. It rained the duration, so inside we stayed, reading and relaxing in the comfort of a beautifully furnished and decorated lodge. We wanted to explore on foot the many sites nearby, but having experienced the scenery from a rocking chair on the large porches, didn't miss it one but. Pat and Phil Cunniffe make you feel right at home and put a breakfast on the table that will wow most anyone…We would recommend this b&b to anyone and we look forward to returning." —GUEST

INNKEEPERS: Pat & Phil Cunniffe
ADDRESS: 2755 Highway 282, Chatsworth, Georgia 30705
TELEPHONE: (706) 695-0920; (800) 695-0905
E-MAIL: hearthstonelodge@alltel.net
WEBSITE: www.thehearthstonelodge.com
ROOMS: 3 Suites; Private baths
CHILDREN: Cannot accommodate
PETS: Not allowed; Resident pet

Croissant French Toast with Soft Caramel Apples

Makes 4 Servings

Batter:
3 large eggs
¼ cup half & half
½ teaspoon pure vanilla extract
Pinch ground cinnamon

Caramel Apples:
½ cup sugar
3 tablespoons unsalted butter
6 Granny Smith apples, peeled,
    cored and cut into ½-inch wedges
½ cup pure maple syrup
3 tablespoons unsalted butter
4 large croissants
Confectioners' sugar for dusting
Ground cinnamon for dusting

For the batter: Whisk together the ingredients until evenly blended. Cover and refrigerate until ready for use.

For the apples: In a dry skillet over medium-low heat, stir sugar constantly with a wooden spoon until the it melts and begins to caramelize (about 5 minutes). Still stirring, add the butter. Once the mixture becomes caramel sauce, fold in the apples. The cool apples may cause the mixture to harden a bit, continue stirring and sauce will warm and smooth once again. When the sauce begins to form around the apples, add the maple syrup. Stir and simmer 10 minutes, until apples are fork tender. Remove from heat but keep warm until ready to serve.

For the French toast: Warm the butter in a large non-stick skillet over medium-low heat. Dredge the croissants in the batter. Lay the croissant in the skillet, cut-side-down, and cook 4-5 minutes. Carefully flip with a spatula and brown the other side. To serve, spoon caramel apples over the bottom half of the croissants and top with the other half. Dust with confectioners' sugar and cinnamon.

SIMMONS-BOND INN B&B

Simmons-Bond Inn B&B, in Toccoa, Georgia, is a perfect example of classical revival Queen Anne Victorian architecture. Built in 1903, the home was intended to be an out-of-town mansion as a gift for wealthy lumberman James B. Simmons's wife. When she expressed that she, a very active society lady, had no intention of living out-of-town, this stately home was squeezed onto a city lot, taking up almost every inch available.

Mrs. Simmons herself was an interesting lady. She kept and milked her own cows and was quite the accomplished cook. She routinely took in boarders including servicemen during WWII and even set up USO tents on the property to entertain paratroopers training at Camp Toccoa. As if that wasn't enough, rumor has it that a storage space under the home's grand staircase may once have been used to store moonshine during the prohibition. Antoinette Mosely Simmons lived in the home until her death in 1954.

INNKEEPER:	Elizabeth Forkey
ADDRESS:	130 West Tugalo Street, Toccoa, Georgia 30577
TELEPHONE:	(706) 282-5183; (877) 658-0746
E-MAIL:	simmonsbond@juno.com
WEBSITE:	www.simmons-bond.com
ROOMS:	5 Rooms; Private baths
CHILDREN:	Welcome
PETS:	Not allowed

Strawberry Stuffed French Toast

Makes 4–6 Servings

"We cooked the Strawberry Stuffed French Toast,
along with several other favorites, when we were featured on the
Southern Hospitality Cooking Show!"

—INNKEEPER, *Simmons-Bond Inn*

1 (8-ounce) package cream cheese, softened
$\frac{1}{3}$ cup powdered sugar
1 teaspoon real vanilla
$\frac{1}{2}$ teaspoon ground cinnamon
8 slices potato or white bread
Fresh strawberries, thinly sliced
3 eggs
$\frac{1}{2}$ cup milk

In a medium bowl, combine the softened cream cheese, powdered sugar, vanilla, and cinnamon. This will be more than enough spread for the recipe; the rest can be stored in the fridge for future use. Spread evenly over all 8 slices of the bread. Place sliced strawberries in an even layer on 4 pieces of bread, top with the other 4 slices of bread to make 4 sandwiches.

In a medium bowl, combine the eggs and milk. Gently dunk the sandwiches in the egg mixture – do not over saturate. Place sandwiches on a heated skillet that has been prepared with butter or cooking spray. Cook over medium heat, turning occasionally, until both sides are a nice golden brow. Serve with strawberry syrup.

Virginia Highland B&B

This fully restored 1920's craftsman bungalow is a surprising treat situated right in the heart of Atlanta. The inn is filled with unique antiques and collectibles acquired by your innkeeper, Adele, on her many world travels. Virginia Highland has three guest rooms – The Victoria, a suite with its own private entrance, antique queen bed, whirlpool tub, and private balcony, the elegant Albert Room, and the private entrance Studio. The inn also has a screened in porch with hammock and breakfast area for warmer months, a dining room with fireplace for more mild mornings, a sunny kitchen with seating space for small parties, and a gorgeous, lush garden with benches, chairs and even a small gazebo, perfect for a lazy afternoon enjoying the sights and sounds of nature.

Breakfast at the Virginia Highland is an ever-changing selection of mouthwatering homemade dishes. Some of Adele's specialties include double cheese omelets, challah French toast, pecan waffles, and banana nut bread. Snacks are available throughout the day as are complimentary beverages and Adele is always more than happy to help with special requests.

INNKEEPER: Adele Northrup

ADDRESS: 630 Orme Circle, N.E., Atlanta, Georgia 30306

TELEPHONE: (404) 892-2735

E-MAIL: adele@virginiahighlandbb.com

WEBSITE: www.virginiahighlandbb.com

ROOMS: 3 Rooms; 1 Suite; Private baths

CHILDREN: Welcome, call ahead

PETS: Not allowed

French Toast Sandwich Surprise

Makes 4 Servings

"Big kids love this dish!"

—INNKEEPER, *Virginia Highland Bed & Breakfast*

4 eggs
½ teaspoon vanilla extract
1 cup fat free half & half
8 slices challah bread
Raw almond butter

In a medium bowl, mix together eggs, vanilla, and half & half. Spread 4 slices of the bread with raw almond butter and top with the remaining 4 slices to make 4 sandwiches, cut each sandwich in half on a diagonal.

Dip sandwiches in the egg mixture and place on a well-buttered and heated skillet or griddle. Cook until both sides are a nice brown. Serve with hot maple syrup.

HOUSE ON SEVENTH B&B

This elegant Queen Anne style home offers gracious and charming accommodations in a homey atmosphere. Period antiques can be found throughout the home, giving it an authentic old Southern feel. Guests will be delighted not only with the inn's tranquil setting, but with the innkeepers' dedication to providing only the best in Southern hospitality.

The inn is perfectly situated near a host of area attractions. At Callaway Gardens, nature lovers will enjoy the butterfly conservatory and nature trails and history buffs can tour the pioneer cabin or travel on to Fort Tyler, the site of an 1865 Civil War battle. Boat rentals are also available at West Point and Harding Lakes.

INNKEEPERS: Ira & Emily Culpepper

ADDRESS: 311 East Seventh Street, West Point, Georgia 31833

TELEPHONE: (706) 645-2064

E-MAIL: info@houseonseventh.com

WEBSITE: www.houseonseventh.com

ROOMS: 3 Rooms; Private baths

CHILDREN: Call ahead

PETS: Not allowed

House on Seventh French Toast

Makes 2 Servings

1 egg
1 cup half and half
1 tablespoon sugar
1 tablespoon cinnamon
¼ teaspoon nutmeg
1 teaspoon orange or lemon extract
3–4 drops vanilla extract
¼ teaspoon salt
6 slices thick white or French bread

In a large bowl, beat together eggs and half and half. Add sugar, cinnamon, nutmeg, orange or lemon extract, vanilla extract, and salt. Soak booth sides of the bread in the mixture for a couple of minutes.

In a large skillet over medium-high heat, fry the battered bread slices in butter until brown on both sides. Serve with strawberries, maple syrup, and a good breakfast sausage.

WISTERIA HALL

Situated on two acres in the heart of historic Washington, Georgia, is a little piece of Southern history. Built in 1795, the home has seen some interesting times. In the 1800s socialite Maria Randolph purchased the home and extended the two-over-two floor plan to include an enormous dining room – the biggest in town – as well as separate ladies' and gentlemen's parlors. It is said that Logan Bleckley, a Chief Justice of the Supreme Court of Georgia, used the home's hidden trap door to hide from the Federals during the Civil War. It is also said that President Woodrow Wilson used to summer here as a child.

Owners Jim and Jane Bundy have painstakingly researched the home's history and restored it to its former splendor. Period antiques including wooden beds and footed tubs grace each of the individually appointed guest rooms. This careful attention to detail along with a dedication to provide top-quality service makes Wisteria Hall the perfect place for relaxing and enjoying the slower, genteel pace the South is famous for.

INNKEEPERS: Jim & Jane Bundy

ADDRESS: 225 East Robert Toombs Avenue, Washington, Georgia 30673

TELEPHONE: (706) 678-7779

E-MAIL: wisteriahall@washingtonwilkes.org

WEBSITE: www.wisteriahallbandb.com

ROOMS: 5 Rooms; Private baths

CHILDREN: Welcome; Call ahead

PETS: Not allowed

Southern French Toast

Makes 8 Servings

Plan ahead, this dish needs to be prepared the night before.

2 tablespoons corn syrup
1 cup firmly packed brown sugar
5 tablespoons butter
16 slices wheat bread, crusts removed
5 eggs
1 cup milk
1 teaspoon vanilla extract
1 cup sour cream
Fresh peaches, thinly sliced
    and sprinkled with sugar*
Toasted pecans

Combine syrup, brown sugar, and butter in a medium sauce-pan. Head, stirring until mixture begins to boil. Pour the syrup mixture into a 9x13-inch pan sprayed with non-stick cooking spray. Nestle bread into syrup making two layers. In a small bowl, combine eggs, milk, and vanilla extract. Pour mixture over bread slices. Cover pan with aluminum foil and refrigerate overnight.

The next morning, preheat oven to 350°F. Remove pan from refrigerator and discard foil. Bake 45 minutes.

To serve: Loosen the edges of bread from the pan with a knife. Invert the pan onto a jelly roll pan so the caramelized syrup is on the top. Cut into serving pieces and top each with a tablespoon of sour cream and sugared peaches. Sprinkle lightly with pecans and serve immediately.

If peaches are not in season, you could substitute apples sautéed in a little butter with pecans and Craisins or you could use sliced strawberries coated with a tablespoon of honey.

Traveler's Rest B&B

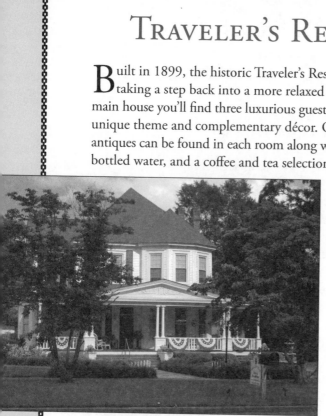

Built in 1899, the historic Traveler's Rest Bed & Breakfast is like taking a step back into a more relaxed and genteel time. In the main house you'll find three luxurious guest rooms, each with its own unique theme and complementary décor. Queen beds and period antiques can be found in each room along with complimentary robes, bottled water, and a coffee and tea selection. For a slight change of pace, the inn's private Carriage House features subtle African décor compliments of your hostess, a native of South Africa.

A mouthwatering breakfast is included with every stay. You can also arrange a candle-lit dinner, light or packed lunches, and even high tea. Make your trip even more romantic and ask for the year-round Be My Valentine Package. This package includes accommodations, a fruit and cheese platter or chocolate covered strawberries on arrival, a special welcoming gift, and a delectable four-course dinner with wine. Adele will also happily arrange a custom package designed especially to suit your needs; all you have to do is ask.

INNKEEPER: Adele Goodman

ADDRESS: 318 North Dooly Street, Montezuma, Georgia 31063

TELEPHONE: (478) 472-0085

E-MAIL: info@travelersrestbb.com

WEBSITE: www.travelersrestbb.com

ROOMS: 1 Room; 2 Suites; 1 Carriage House; Private baths

CHILDREN: Welcome, call ahead

PETS: Welcome

French Toast Soufflé

Makes 2 Servings

"Wonderful for honeymooners or anniversaries!"
—INNKEEPER, *Traveler's Rest B&B*

4–5 slices day-old white bread
8–10 chocolate chips (optional)
⅓ cup milk
4 eggs
½ teaspoon baking powder
1 teaspoon vanilla essence
2 tablespoons sugar
2 tablespoons cinnamon sugar
Powdered sugar to decorate

Preheat oven to 450°F. Spray 2 heart-shaped ramekins with non-stick cooking spray. Remove crusts from bread and cut into cubes; pack the cubes into the ramekins. If using the chocolate chips, bury them among the bread cubes. In a small bowl, beat together the eggs, milk, sugar, baking powder, and vanilla essence. Pour the egg mixture over the bread cubes and sprinkle with cinnamon sugar. Bake until puffed and golden brown, approximately 20 minutes.

Garnish with powdered sugar and serve immediately with warm syrup.

MAGNOLIA HALL B&B

This beautifully restored 1880s Victorian-style home sits on one acre of lush land just a few minutes' walk from Hamilton's town square. Magnolia Hall was originally constructed between the years of 1880 and 1882 as a wedding gift for Beth Callaway's (of nearby Callaway Gardens resort) grandparents. Although the home has been completely renovated in the years since, owners Dale and Ken are sure the newlyweds would approve and many of their own descendants have visited the bed & breakfast themselves.

"Leslie and I have thoroughly enjoyed spending our 'get-away' time with you kind folks... The food was delicious and the preparation and hospitality was exemplary. We will be back and we will bring our family and friends..." —GUEST

INNKEEPERS: Dale & Ken Smith

ADDRESS: 127 Barnes Mill Road, Hamilton, Georgia 31811

TELEPHONE: (706) 628-4566; (877) 813-4394

E-MAIL: kgsmag@juno.com

WEBSITE: www.magnoliahallbb.com

ROOMS: 3 Rooms; 2 Suites; Private baths

CHILDREN: Children age 12 and older welcome

PETS: Not allowed; Resident cat

Georgia Croissant

Makes 1 Serving

"This is one of our guest favorites!
In Georgia, we do love our peaches!"
—INNKEEPER, *Magnolia Hall Bed & Breakfast*

1 large croissant
1 tablespoon good peach preserves
2 fork beaten eggs
½ teaspoon almond flavoring
1 cup half & half
2 fresh peaches, sliced
Whipped topping
Toasted almonds

Preheat oven to 400°F. Split the croissant and spread preserves over the bottom. In a bowl, mix the eggs, almond flavoring, and half & half. Dip the croissant halves into the mixture, cut-side-down, then press the halves back together.

Place the croissant on a lightly sprayed pan and bake 10 minutes. To serve, top with well sugared peaches, whipped topping, and almonds.

Seventy-Four Ranch B&B

This working ranch and b&b offers guests a unique lodging and vacation experience. Visitors are invited to ride the ranch's expansive 1,200 acres, learn to rope cows, or even fish for their dinner.

At night you can roast marshmallows while enjoying true campfire tales of the inn's history. If you like, you can even camp on the ranch's grounds and wake to enjoy a hearty breakfast and hot shower at the inn.

The ranch offers guests a wide array of accommodations to choose from. There are two guest rooms in the main house each with its own private balcony, kitchenette, claw-foot tub, and vaulted cedar ceilings. The porch cabin offers guests a fenced side yard, swing, and chiminea. The saddle house is perfect for families and features four double bunk beds, a large game table, and is stocked with toys and games. Finally, the 1832 cabin features a handmade cedar double bed, cedar ceiling, stack stone chimney, and kitchen stocked with authentic tin cookware for a true 1800's cabin experience.

INNKEEPERS: Larry & Pam Butler
ADDRESS: 9205 Highway 53 West, Jasper, Georgia 30143
TELEPHONE: (706) 692-0123
E-MAIL: reservations@seventyfourranch.com
WEBSITE: www.seventyfourranch.com
ROOMS: 2 Rooms; 1 Suite; 3 Cabins; Private & shared baths
CHILDREN: Welcome
PETS: Welcome; Resident pets

Orange Tangerine Pecan French Toast

Makes 8-10 Servings

Plan ahead, you'll need to begin preparations on this dish the night before.

1 cup brown sugar
1/3 cup butter, melted
2 tablespoons corn syrup
1/3 cup pecan pieces
1 loaf hearty white bread
1/2 tablespoon orange zest
1/2 cup orange juice
1/2 cup tangerine juice
1/2 cup milk
3 tablespoons sugar
1 teaspoon cinnamon
1 teaspoon vanilla

3 egg whites
2 eggs

Syrup:
1 cup sugar 1/2 tablespoon
  tangerine zest
1/2 cup water
1/2 cup orange juice
1/4 cup tangerine juice
1 tablespoon corn starch
2 tablespoons unsalted butter

For French toast: In a medium bowl, mix together brown sugar, melted butter, and corn syrup; pour mixture into a greased 9x13-inch pan. Sprinkle pecans over mixture. Arrange bread slices over the pecans. In a medium bowl, whisk together remaining French toast ingredients and pour over bread, pressing down. Cover and refrigerate overnight. The following morning, preheat oven to 350°F. Allow dish to sit at room temperature for 20 minutes before baking 30 minutes. To serve, invert so that pecans are on top and serve with syrup.

For syrup: In a small saucepan, bring sugar and water to a boil, stirring until sugar has melted. In a small bowl, combine juices and cornstarch; add to sugar mixture and simmer 6-8 minutes. Add the butter and stir until it melts. Pour over French toast.

Homemade Peanut Butter &
Bananas Foster Breakfast Panini

Makes 4 Servings

*"This recipe is an adaptation and combination
of two recipes from Williams Sonoma."*

—INNKEEPER, *Seventy-Four Ranch Bed & Breakfast*

Peanut Butter:
2 cups unsalted, roasted peanuts
½ cup peanut oil
1 teaspoon salt
2 teaspoons honey

Bananas Foster:
2 tablespoons butter
2 large ripe bananas, sliced
2 tablespoons brown sugar
½ teaspoon rum or imitation rum flavoring

8 slices of bread of choice

For the peanut butter: Mix all ingredients in a food processor until mixture has reached desired consistency – you will have to scrape sides down intermittently. Extra can be stored for later use.

For bananas foster: In a sauté pan, melt the butter; sauté bananas. Add the sugar and cook until bananas are slightly softened. Add rum or rum flavoring.

For the panini: Coat a panini grill with high-heat spray, such as canola. Spread 4 slices of bread with the peanut butter and 4 slices with the banana mixture. Press 1 peanut butter slice with 1 banana slice to make a sandwich, repeat to make 4 total. Grill each sandwich on the panini grill or spray a fry pan and place a heavy skillet on top of the sandwiches while cooking, flipping when the bottom is lightly browned.

Peaches N' Cream Waffles

Makes 4–6 Servings

"This is an original spin
on the standard buttermilk waffle recipe."
—INNKEEPER, *Seventy-Four Ranch Bed & Breakfast*

Use your favorite buttermilk waffle recipe, or mix
2 ounces softened cream cheese
5 peach slices, finely diced
½ cup crushed pecans

Mix your favorite buttermilk waffle recipe, or mix, for up to
6 servings. Add the cream cheese, peaches and pecans. You may
need to add extra waffle mix for consistency. Pour the batter into
a waffle maker and repeat until you have used up the batter.

To serve, garnish with sliced peaches, pecans, butter, and hot
maple syrup.

OLDE SAVANNAH

The elegant and historic Olde Savannah Inn is recognized as one of the most distinguished inns in all of Savannah. Impeccable service, stately décor, and charming Southern hospitality are just some of the things you will find at this luxurious inn. Each of the inn's four guest rooms has a unique theme with complementary color schemes and antiques. Amenities include the highest quality linens and towels, luxury bath products, complimentary wine social, and a gourmet breakfast.

"...Absolutely every detail in this home is the best. No Corners have been cut anywhere. Everything is exquisite, fabulous, amazing, and beautiful. You will be surrounded in wonderfully sumptuous luxury, coupled with such lovely hospitality that you won't want to ever leave...Andy and I have both traveled extensively. We've been fortunate enough to stay in many five star hotels and our stay at The Olde Savannah Inn was far and above the best experience ever. You have the best of everything and the most charming, elegant, caring people so happy to meet your every wish...you could not ask for more." —GUEST

INNKEEPER: Kathleen Dupuis

ADDRESS: 217 East Gaston Street, Savannah, Georgia 31401

TELEPHONE: (912) 247-8254

E-MAIL: info@theoldesavannahinn.com

WEBSITE: www.theoldesavannahinn.com

ROOMS: 4 Rooms; Private baths

CHILDREN: Children age 12 and older welcome

PETS: Not allowed

The Olde Savannah Inn's Famous Blueberry Pancakes

"Guests love these pancakes. New guests request this favorite after reading Tripadvisor's Rave Reviews."

—INNKEEPER, *The Olde Savannah Inn*

4 cups all-purpose flour
4 cups buttermilk
2 teaspoons baking powder
2 teaspoons baking soda
4 tablespoons pure vanilla extract
4 tablespoons pure almond extract
1 teaspoon salt
4 tablespoons sugar
4 large eggs, separated
8 tablespoons sweetened butter, melted
1 pint fresh or frozen blueberries, rinsed and drained

In a large bowl, combine flour, buttermilk, baking powder, baking soda, vanilla and almond extracts, salt, sugar, and egg yolks. Mix in butter using a hand mixer until the dough consistency is smooth. In a small bowl, whisk egg whites until they are bubbly. Carefully fold egg whites and blueberries into pancake batter.

Pour ¼-cupful of batter onto a heated skillet or griddle. Flip pancake when the edges begin to bubble and cook until lightly browned. Serve with apple smoked bacon and sausage.

Azalea Inn & Gardens

The turn-of-the-century Azalea Inn & Gardens sits on one of the original plots colonized by British and European settlers in the early 1700s. Today, the inn retains its original Old-South charm with its gorgeously appointed "Southern-style" suites and guest rooms,

and its vintage eco-friendly gardens. This casual bed & breakfast prides itself on its laid-back atmosphere and relaxing setting and was voted one of the most romantic inns in all of Savannah.

The mild Savannah weather makes the Azalea Inn a great place to visit regardless of the season, and guests are sure to find plenty to amuse themselves in the surrounding area. The grounds feature a swimming pool and courtyard as well as balconies and verandahs perfect for a relaxing afternoon. Nearby attractions include Savannah's historic garden district, Forsyth Park, and the Mansion on Forsyth art gallery. You can take one of the many walking tours around the area or book a romantic historic carriage tour.

INNKEEPERS: Teresa & Micheal Jacobson

ADDRESS: 217 East Huntingdon Street, Savannah, Georgia 31401

TELEPHONE: (912) 236-2707; (800) 582-3823

E-MAIL: azalea.inn@comcast.net

WEBSITE: www.azaleainn.com

ROOMS: 7 Suites; 2 Cottages; Private & shared baths

CHILDREN: Children age 12 and older welcome

PETS: Not allowed; Resident pets

Buttermilk Pecan Pancakes

Makes 4 Servings

"These pancakes are light and moist; the texture is a cross between a crêpe and a pancake."

—INNKEEPER, *The Azalea Inn*

1 cup all-purpose flour

2 tablespoons yellow cornmeal

2 tablespoons packed golden brown sugar

1 teaspoon baking powder

1 teaspoon baking soda

½ teaspoon salt

1 cup buttermilk

1 cup plain whole-milk yogurt

1 large egg

Additional unsalted butter

1 cup chopped pecans

In a large bowl, combine flour, cornmeal, brown sugar, baking powder, baking soda, and salt. In a separate medium bowl, whisk together buttermilk, yogurt, and egg; add to the dry ingredients and stir until just blended but still lumpy. Gently mix in 1½ tablespoons of melted butter. Avoid overmixing the batter (it's okay if there are lumps) to ensure that the pancakes will be airy.

Heat a griddle or large non-stick skillet over medium heat. Spread a thin coating of butter over the griddle and allow to melt. Working in batches, drop batter by ⅓-cupsful onto the griddle, spacing apart. Cook until brown on bottom and bubbles form on top, about 3 minutes. Turn pancakes over and sprinkle with chopped pecans. Cook until bottoms are brown and pancakes are barely firm to touch.

THE BRADY INN

Whether your interests are football, golf, historic homes, or a leisurely weekend browsing for antiques, the Brady Inn B&B is ready to pamper you in classic southern comfort. The Brady Inn is made up of two Victorian era homes, each lovingly restored to their original grace and splendor. Heart pine floors, Victorian mantels, and period décor are featured throughout the inn.

The home-away-from-home atmosphere will make even the weariest travelers feel welcome and relaxed. The inn even offers up its expansive lawns and covered porches for your special event, whether is be a family reunion, or an intimate dinner for two.

INNKEEPERS: Karen & Peter Wibell

ADDRESS: 250 North Second Street, Madison, Georgia 30650

TELEPHONE: (706) 342-4400

E-MAIL: host@bradyinn.com

WEBSITE: www.bradyinn.com

ROOMS: 7 Rooms; Private baths

CHILDREN: Welcome

PETS: Not allowed

Brady Inn Strawberry Banana Pancakes

Makes 7–8 Servings

*"Guests staying multiple nights tend to expect
a pancake breakfast. This is a favored preparation."*

—INNKEEPER, *The Brady Inn*

2 cups all-purpose flour
2 teaspoons baking powder
½ teaspoon baking soda
½ teaspoon salt
¼ cup sugar
4 large eggs
1¾ cups buttermilk
¼ cup melted butter
Canola oil
½ cup ripe bananas, mashed
½ cup diced strawberries
Confectioners' sugar
Maple syrup

In a mixing bowl, combine flour, baking powder, baking soda, salt, and sugar. In a separate bowl, blend eggs, buttermilk, and melted butter. Pour the liquid mixture into the center of the dry mixture and blend by hand until evenly moist. Heat a griddle over medium-high heat for approximately 5 minutes. Wipe the surface with canola oil using a paper towel. Just before cooking, fold bananas and strawberries into the batter.

Drop batter onto griddle – a little less that ¼ cup per pancake – allowing room for batter to spread and not touch the other pancakes. Cook until small bubbles appear on top surface (about 2 minutes) turn pancake over and cook for approximately 1–2 additional minutes. Pancakes should have a golden-brown color, so adjust heat as needed. Serve three pancakes per plate; dust with confectioners' sugar and serve with real maple syrup and fresh sausage patties or bacon slices. Garnish with strawberry halves.

THE FORSYTH PARK INN

The circa 1893 Forsyth Park Inn is one of Savannah's most elegant and historic inns. Southern hospitality and charm abound in this magnificent Victorian b&b. Guests will wake to a sumptuous, gourmet breakfast each morning, will enjoy wine and hors d'oeuvres each afternoon, and a baked sweet with tea and coffee in the evening.

The inn also offers guests special package options that include spa treatments, local ghost tours, dinner certificates at fine-dining restaurants, and afternoon tea. While away the afternoon relaxing on the verandah in one of the inn's many rocking chairs, walk through the elegant gardens, or wander through the majestic Forsyth ark. Whatever you choose, the Forsyth Park Inn is dedicated to making each guest's stay a memorable one.

INNKEEPERS: Rick & Lori Blass

ADDRESS: 102 West Hall Street, Savannah, Georgia 31401

TELEPHONE: (912) 233-6804

E-MAIL: innkeeper@forsythparkinn.com

WEBSITE: www.forsythparkinn.com

ROOMS: 11 Rooms; 1 Cottage; Private baths

CHILDREN: Children age 12 and older welcome

PETS: Welcome; Call ahead; Resident pets

Orange Ricotta Pancakes

Makes 8 Servings

"This recipe was adapted from Bon Appetit *magazine and Ms. Ozella's kitchen. It's a true guest favorite!"*

—INNKEEPER, *Forsyth Inn*

2 tablespoons orange zest
2 oranges, juiced
1¾ cups ricotta cheese
2 eggs
1 cup self-rising flour
⅓ cup sugar
1 teaspoon baking powder
Powdered sugar, to serve
Maple syrup, to serve

Zest and juice the oranges. In a large bowl, mix together the zest, juice, ricotta cheese, and eggs. In a separate bowl, sift together the flour, sugar, and baking powder. Mix the dry ingredients into the wet mixture until well combined. Ladle 3–4 tablespoons of batter onto a hot griddle and cook until golden brown. These pancakes are very delicate and you may want to use a large spatula to flip and remove them.

Sprinkle pancakes with powdered sugar and serve with maple syrup.

MOUNTAIN LAUREL CREEK
INN & SPA

The rustic and charming Mountain Laurel Creek Inn & Spa is so much more than a regular bed & breakfast! Each of the inn's elegant guest rooms features unique décor coupled with luxury accommodations including gas fireplaces and whirlpool tubs

big enough for two as well as private balconies with breathtaking views. Pamper yourself with a spa day at the inn's Oasis Spa. Here you can enjoy hot stone massages, reflexology, and a host of facial treatments.

"This bed and breakfast is AMAZING! We came for an overnight and wish we could have stayed a week. The rooms are so comfortable and luxurious. We fell in love with this inn, and the town as well. The hospitality and overall atmosphere was more than we could have asked for or expected. The best compliment we can give is that we will be counting the days until we can get back!" —GUEST

INNKEEPERS: Dennis Hoover & David Mulcahy

ADDRESS: 202 Talmer Grizzle Road, Dahlonega, Georgia 30533

TELEPHONE: (706) 867-8134

E-MAIL: info@mountainlaurelcreek.com

WEBSITE: www.mountainlaurelcreek.com

ROOMS: 5 Suites; Private baths

CHILDREN: Cannot accommodate

PETS: Not allowed

German Apple Pancakes

Makes 4 Servings

"This is one of our house favorites. Guests just love them and request them all the time. You make the batter the night before and leave in the refrigerator, or make in the morning and let batter rest at least an hour and a half before using."

—INNKEEPER, *Mountain Laurel Creek Inn & Spa*

5 eggs
⅓ cup flour
½ cup milk (can substitute soy milk)
½ teaspoon vanilla
¼ pound butter
½ teaspoon cinnamon
¼ teaspoon nutmeg
½ teaspoon baking powder
⅓ cup sugar
1 Granny Smith apple

Sugar Mix:
⅓ cup sugar
½ teaspoon cinnamon
¼ teaspoon nutmeg

In a large bowl, beat together the eggs and flour; add the remaining ingredients, except the apples, and mix well. Cover and refrigerate batter overnight. In the morning, remove from fridge.

Preheat oven to 350°F. Place a 12-inch ovenproof frying pan on the stove. Peel the apple and slice thinly. Melt the butter in the pan; sprinkle with ½ of the sugar mix then lay the apples on top in a single layer. Sprinkle with the remaining sugar mix and cook until sugar melts and begins to bubble. Pour batter over the top and place pan in oven. Bake 30 minutes. Remove the pan from oven and cut pancake into 4 slices. Sprinkle with powdered sugar and serve with whipped cream, syrup, and sausage. Garnish with orange slices.

LAFAYETTE MANOR INN

Lafayette Manor offers vacationers AAA 3-Diamond accommodations in a gorgeous antebellum, Federal-Style manse. The home was originally built in 1819 in the "two over two" style that was popular in the day. Since then, the home has been fully renovated and expanded to house a total of seven guest rooms. Each room is elegantly appointed with crystal, fine antiques, and oriental rugs. The inn also has a private cottage with kitchenette and porch available to guests.

Downtown Washington, Georgia is just a short stroll from the hotel. This historic town has over 100 antebellum, colonial, and Victorian homes! Tour the area and take in the sites, tour the Calloway mansion, visit the WWII museum, shop, and enjoy a light meal in town – save room, though, Lafayette Manor offers a delectable five-course dinner option.

INNKEEPERS: Guillaume & Sokunvathany Slama

ADDRESS: 219 East Robert Toombs Avenue, Washington, Georgia 30673

TELEPHONE: (706) 678-5922

E-MAIL: info@lafayettemanor.com

WEBSITE: http://lafayettemanor.com

ROOMS: 7 Rooms; 1 Suite; 1 Cottage; Private baths

CHILDREN: Children age 8 and older welcome

PETS: Dogs allowed; Resident pets

Apple Crêpes

Makes 4 Servings

"Remember, crêpes are thin, pancakes are thick. You can also make them a bit larger, then roll them and top the sauce over them. Serve for breakfast or with afternoon tea."

—INNKEEPER, *Lafayette Manor*

2 Granny Smith apples
2 eggs
1¾ ounce sugar
1¾ ounces melted butter
2½ ounces flour
1¾ ounce almond meal
Zest from 1 lemon
1¾ ounce butter

Sauce:
2½ ounces honey
1 ounce fresh cream (or sour cream)

For the crêpes: Peel and grate the apples. Break the eggs into a medium bowl, add the sugar and whip until the mixture whitens. Keep whipping and add the melted butter, flour, lemon zest, and almond meal. Gently incorporate the grated apples. Melt some butter in a large, non-stick frying pan. Pour a large tablespoon of batter into each corner of the pan, so as to have 4 crêpes. The mixture should spread gently to form little round crêpes. Cook over a gently heat for 2 minutes, then flip the crêpes and cook for another 2 minutes. Keep the cooked crêpes on a warm plate before serving. Top with the honey sauce and serve.

For the sauce: Pour the honey into a saucepan and caramelize it over medium heat. Add the cream and whip until smooth and creamy.

Maison LaVigne

Maison LaVigne, a luxury bed & breakfast located in historic Hapeville, Georgia, just minutes from downtown Atlanta, is a haven for vacationers seeking an intimate and romantic getaway. Owner Eileen Randman's top-quality, personalized service has drawn

comparison to that of the most elite resorts. The inn's combination of genteel charm and French Provincial décor perfectly compliments the laid-back hospitality and down-home feel of the inn.

Of course, no b&b would be complete without the food. Randman, a professionally trained chef, delights visitors' palates with her seasonal menus. A hot and hearty breakfast is included with every stay. Randman also offers a classic High Tea, available to guests by reser-vation. Selections include an assortment of traditional tea sandwiches, home-made pastries and petit fours, and even a vegetarian quiche. Private dinners and luncheons can also be arranged for your special event. And, as if that weren't enough, private cooking classes are also available by request.

INNKEEPER: Eileen Randman

ADDRESS: 3532 South Fulton Avenue, Hapeville, Georgia 30354

TELEPHONE: (404) 766-5561

E-MAIL: atableoffriends@aol.com

WEBSITE: www.maisonlavigne.com

ROOMS: 3 Rooms; Private baths

CHILDREN: Welcome; Call ahead

PETS: Welcome; Resident pets

Crêpes

Makes 4 Servings

2 cups sifted flour
  (King Arthur brand recommended)
½ teaspoon fine sea salt
4 eggs
1 cup cold milk
1 cup cold water
Melted butter, cooled

Measure the dry ingredients into a large bowl. In a separate medium bowl, whisk together the eggs milk, and water. Blend the wet mixture into the flour mixture. Pour in the cooled butter and blend until smooth. Place the crêpe "batter" in the fridge and allow to rest at least 1–2 minutes.

Have a hot, thin, non-stick pan, a heat-proof rubber spatula, a silicone brush, and clarified butter or olive oil standing by. Heat the pan with a bit of butter or oil and make a tester crêpe. Pour the batter into the pan, quickly swirl and cook the first side all the way through. If you can turn the crêpe with your fingers, this is the best, if not, flip with the rubber spatula and continue cooking until second side is done. Repeat until the batter is used up.

STONEHURST PLACE

Stonehurst Place combines exemplary service with Southern hospitality and charm. You'll feel as though you're staying in a grand hotel, while receiving the personalized attention that only a b&b can provide.

The quaint and cozy Stonehurst Place was originally built in 1896. The home remained with the same family for over a century and, as a result, has retained many of its original turn-of-the-century charms. Owner Barb Shadomy has lovingly restored the home to its original splendor, and added some modern touches that have made the home more eco-friendly and energy efficient. With its lovely gardens and its serene setting, you'll almost forget that you're just a short walk away from Atlanta's theater, museum, and arts district!

INNKEEPER: Rose Marie Ray

ADDRESS: 923 Piedmont Avenue, NE, Atlanta, Georgia 30309

TELEPHONE: (404) 881-0722

E-MAIL: info@stonehurstplace.com

WEBSITE: www.stonehurstplace.com

ROOMS: 1 Room; 1 Suite

CHILDREN: Welcome; Call ahead

PETS: Small dogs welcome; Call ahead

Stonehurst Place Crêpes

Makes up to 10 Crêpes

4 large eggs
1 cup milk
1 cup water, plus droplets if needed
1 teaspoon salt
4 tablespoons oil
1 cup Wondra flour or instant-blending flour

In a medium bowl, beat the eggs; add in liquids, salt and oil. Gradually beat in the flour – a blender is ideal for this. Refrigerate the batter for 20–30 minutes, or overnight. Return batter to room temperature before using.

Heat a crêpe or non-stick skillet over medium-high heat. Brush on a small amount of oil for the first crêpe. While the oil is heating stack some waxed paper next to a plate for separating the finished crêpes. Add a small ladleful of batter to the pan and cook until bubbles for on the surface and the bottom is brown. Flip the crêpe and cook for an additional 15–20 seconds then slide onto the waxed paper. Repeat until all the batter has been used.

To serve Stonehurst Place special crêpes: Sauté leeks, white parts only. Scramble eggs, as needed. Wrap the eggs and sautéed leeks in a crêpe and place in an oven-safe dish. Top with cubed ham or bacon, chopped tomatoes, and grated Gruyère or Swiss cheese. Place under a broiler just until the cheese has lightly browned.

Egg & Breakfast Entrées

Egg & Breakfast Entrées

> "All food is the gift of the gods
> and has something of the miraculous,
>
> the egg no less than the truffle."
>
> —Sybille Bedford

1884 Paxton House Inn

The elegant and romantic 1884 Paxton Inn was featured on the first tourism brochures encouraging Northerners to travel south for winter season vacations. This Victorian bed & breakfast is known for its Southern charm and hospitality and has played host to all manner of guests since reopening its doors in 1991. The luxurious accommodations and welcoming atmosphere make this the perfect romantic getaway and a great place for travelers seeking something more personal and inviting than the same old hotel.

Guests will begin each day with a splendid breakfast made from quality ingredients, using family recipes that have been passed down through the generations. With historic plantations, a nature conservancy, fishing, museums, and great antique shops all nearby, guests are sure to find something new and exciting to occupy their time in Thomasville.

INNKEEPER: Susie M. Sherrod

ADDRESS: 445 Remington Avenue, Thomasville, Georgia 31792

TELEPHONE: (229) 226-5197

E-MAIL: 1884@rose.net

WEBSITE: www.1884paxtonhouseinn.com

ROOMS: 2 Rooms; 5 Suites; 2 Cottages; Private baths

CHILDREN: Children age 12 and older welcome

PETS: Not allowed

1884 Paxton House Inn
Grand Eggs

Makes 1 Serving

"Repeat guests request this dish as soon as they check in."

—INNKEEPER, *1884 Paxton House Inn*

1 (1-ounce) slice chopped Smithfield Ham
½ cup shredded Mexican cheese blend
2 eggs, beaten
1 tablespoon heavy cream
Grated Parmesan cheese
Paprika

Preheat convection oven to 325°F (standard oven 350°F). Spray one oval ramekin with non-stick spray. Spread chopped ham in the bottom of the ramekin, top with Mexican cheese blend. Beat together the eggs and heavy cream and pour over cheese.

Place the ramekin on a sheet pan in the center of the preheated oven. Bake 12–16 minutes, or until set — watch carefully so as not to overcook. Remove from oven and sprinkle with Parmesan cheese and paprika. Serve immediately.

McKinnon House B&B

Situated in the heart of Old Town Brunswick, the McKinnon House Bed & Breakfast is the perfect place to experience the charm and hospitality of the old South. This Victorian home was originally built in 1902 as the residence of a local lumber magnate. Current owner, Jo Miller, purchased the home in 1993 and transformed it into a breathtaking and gorgeous b&b complete with family heirlooms and period antiques. A gourmet breakfast

 is included with every guest's stay and complimentary afternoon refreshments are served daily in the inn's parlor.

McKinnon House is conveniently located just minutes from the Golden Isle resorts as well as both St. Simons Island and Jekyll Isle where guests can lounge on one of the many beaches, rent a sailboat for the day, enjoy some of the best fishing in the area, or just enjoy the scenery. Historic Brunswick features a wide array of specialty shops, restaurants and cafes, antique shops, and art galleries.

INNKEEPER: Jo Miller

ADDRESS: 1001 Egmont Street, Brunswick, Georgia 31520

TELEPHONE: (912) 261-9100; (866) 261-9100

E-MAIL: N/A

WEBSITE: www.mckinnonhousebandb.com

ROOMS: 2 Rooms; 1 Suite; Private baths

CHILDREN: Children age 10 and older welcome

PETS: Call ahead

Toasted Egg Cups

Makes 6 Servings

"This recipe was adapted from Amy Vanderbilt's Complete
Cookbook. *It is very close to the recipe my grandmother used to make
what she called 'Egg Cups' when I was a little girl. Unfortunately,
her exact recipe went with her when she died in the 70s at age 99.
This has been a favorite with guests at McKinnon House
for over ten years."*

—INNKEEPER, *McKinnon House Bed & Breakfast*

6 slices bread
1 stick melted butter
6 eggs
¼ cup milk
1 teaspoon salt
1 teaspoon green onion
¼ cup grated sharp Cheddar cheese
   plus more for sprinkling

Preheat oven to 350°F. Remove crusts from bread; brush both
sides with melted butter. Gently press each slice into one section
of a muffin tin. In a medium bowl, beat eggs with milk, salt, onion,
and cheese. Divide the egg mixture equally between the bread
cups. Set muffin tin in a shallow pan containing a little water.
Bake 30 minutes. Serve two egg cups per plate.

Add fresh ground pepper, dry mustard, or other spices for variety.
You can also add ham, shrimp, or bacon to the egg mixture before
baking.

MAGNOLIA HALL B&B

M agnolia Hall is a charming bed & breakfast located just minutes from historic Hamilton, Georgia's town square. Each of the inn's five cozy guest rooms has its own unique décor complete with heart-pine floors, lace curtains, and antique period furnishings. A scrumptious candlelight breakfast is served each morning and a

basket of Dale's homemade goodies comes with each room. Southern hospitality and pampering service are just par for the course at Magnolia Hall B&B, so it's easy to see how the inn earned its Three Diamond rating as well as its place on the 2004 list of Top 15 B&B Inns in North America.

The inn sits amidst one-acre of lovely gardens and fragrant magnolia trees. The covered porch with its swing and rockers is just the place for a relaxing afternoon spent enjoying the scenery and sipping a glass of sweet tea – just like they did in the good old days.

INNKEEPERS: Dale & Ken Smith

ADDRESS: 127 Barnes Mill Road, Hamilton, Georgia 31811

TELEPHONE: (706) 628-4566; (877) 813-4394

E-MAIL: kgsmag@juno.com

WEBSITE: www.magnoliahallbb.com

ROOMS: 3 Rooms; 2 Suites; Private baths

CHILDREN: Children age 12 and older welcome

PETS: Not allowed; Resident cat

Baked Egg From Magnolia Hall

Makes 1 Serving

Mazola vegetable spray
1 tablespoon evaporated milk
1 fork beaten egg
Dash seasoned salt
Grated Havarti cheese
Parsley

Preheat oven to 425·F. Spray an oven-proof custard dish with vegetable spray. Put the evaporated milk into the dish; pour in the egg. Add the seasoned salt and cover the egg with the grated Havarti.

Place the custard dish on a cookie sheet and bake for 12–15 minutes until the egg puffs up. Remove the egg from the dish and sprinkle with parsley. Serve over grits.

Mountain
Memories B&B

Mountain Memories is known for their special "skip lunch" breakfast buffet. This hearty buffet includes items such as biscuits, maple pecan pancakes, and French toast - all heart shaped, of course. They also have an egg dish du jour, Southern biscuits and

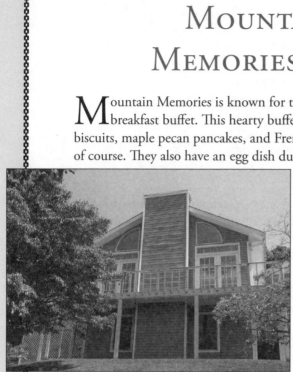

gravy, fresh fruit, and their signature coffee cake. Each evening, they offer a dessert buffet before bedtime. You can enjoy homemade dessert items by candlelight while basking in the spectacular mountain view.

As a special afternoon treat, ask for one of the inn's hand-packed picnic baskets. You and your special someone can choose from the Old Fashioned Southern basket, the French Flair basket, the Simpler Time, or the Not-A-Stallion Italian basket. Each basket comes with themed meal selections and, with the exception of the appropriately named Simpler Time, each also comes with napkins, silverware, china, a cloth tablecloth, and candles.

INNKEEPERS: Bill & TooToo Cirlot
ADDRESS: 385 Chancey Drive, Hiawassee, Georgia 30546
TELEPHONE: (706) 896-8439; (800) 335-8439
E-MAIL: mtnmem@brmemc.net
WEBSITE: www.mountainmemoriesbandb.com
ROOMS: 6 Rooms; 3 Cabins; Private baths
CHILDREN: Children age 14 and older welcome
PETS: Welcome; Call ahead; Resident pets

Italian Baked Eggs

Makes 6–8 Servings

12 large eggs
8 ounces softened cream cheese
2 cups grated mozzarella cheese
½ cup grated Parmesan cheese
½ cup cottage cheese
½ cup blue cheese
⅓ cup white wine
2 tablespoons Italian herb seasoning mix
1 teaspoon crushed red pepper
2 teaspoons dried mustard
2 teaspoons garlic powder
1 teaspoon onion powder
½ teaspoon baking powder
¼ cup flour

Preheat oven to 350°F. In a large bowl, beat the eggs with a hand mixer. Add the cream cheese and beat again. Add the remaining ingredients and beat until well blended. Pour the mixture into a 9x13-inch baking dish and bake 40–45 minutes until lightly browned.

Southwest variation: Follow the same instructions as with the Italian eggs, using the same amount of eggs, cream cheese, cottage cheese, garlic powder, onion powder, mustard, flour, and baking powder. To this, add 2½–3 cups grated Cheddar cheese, 2 teaspoons lime juice, ¼ cup tequila, 1 teaspoon chipotle seasoning, 2 teaspoons chili powder, and 2 teaspoons cumin.

1842 Inn

This unique inn sits on two lush acres in beautiful Macon, Georgia. The original building, a Greek revival, antebellum home, was built in 1842 by John Gresham, a former mayor of Macon. The Victorian Cottage was moved to the property in 1983, expanding the inn to a total of 19 stately appointed guest rooms. There are also four parlors, a courtyard with gardens for entertaining, and a seventeen-column veranda. Of course, what Southern home would be complete without the requisite porch for relaxing and drinking iced tea? The 1842 Inn has multiple porches just for this purpose.

Guests will enjoy a hearty complimentary breakfast each morning and can choose to be served in their guest room, in the parlor, or in the courtyard. The inn also offers chauffeur service for dinner in town. With the amenities of a grand hotel and the ambience of a country inn, the 1842 Inn is the perfect place for a relaxing and romantic stay in historic Macon, Georgia.

INNKEEPER: Nazario Filipponi

ADDRESS: 353 College Street, Macon, Georgia 31201

TELEPHONE: (877) 452-6599

E-MAIL: management@1842inn.com

WEBSITE: www.1842inn.com

ROOMS: 19 Rooms; Private baths

CHILDREN: Welcome

PETS: Call ahead

Plantation Casserole

Makes 1 Serving

2–3 slices bacon
Shredded cheese of choice
2 eggs
$\frac{1}{3}$ cup heavy whipping cream
Pinch garlic
Salt, to taste
1 teaspoon minced onion
Mrs. Dash, to taste

Preheat oven to 350°F and spray one ramekin with non-stick cooking spray. Cook and drain the bacon and break into small pieces. Lay the bacon and shredded cheese into the bottom of the ramekin – enough cheese to cover the bottom. In a small bowl, mix together the eggs, whipped cream, garlic, salt, onion, and Mrs. Dash; pour mixture over the bacon and cheese. Bake 20–25 minutes until egg mixture is done.

BROUGHTON STREET GUEST HOUSE

Located in the heart of historic Savannah, Georgia is the elegant and luxurious Broughton Street Guest House. One look around this gorgeous inn and you'll feel as though you've taken a step back in time. The inn offers a private carriage house and three unique guest rooms including the aptly named Library Room. Each room

features period antiques and Edwardian décor.

Just a short walk away, guests will find a plethora of art and antique galleries, museums, craft stores, and fine-dining restaurants. Historic Savannah ghost tours and River Street carriage rides as well as riverboat and trolley tours can be found nearby as well.

INNKEEPER: Robbie Bell
ADDRESS: 511 East Broughton Street, Savannah, Georgia 31401
TELEPHONE: (912) 232-6633
E-MAIL: reservations@broughtonst.com
WEBSITE: www.broughtonst.com
ROOMS: 4 Rooms; Private & shared baths
CHILDREN: Welcome
PETS: Not allowed

Breakfast Casserole

Makes 6 Servings

"This recipe was given to me by a friend.
It uses simple ingredients and is easy to prepare."

—INNKEEPER, *Broughton Street Guest House*

3 cups frozen hash brown potatoes
1 pound sausage, cooked, drained, and crumbled
¾ cup chopped green peppers
¾ cup chopped onion
3 cups shredded cheese of choice
1 dozen eggs, slightly beaten with 2 cups milk

Preheat oven to 350°F. Layer ingredients in a large casserole dish and bake for 50 minutes.

All but the eggs can be prepared in advance for quick preparation.

BEACH BED & BREAKFAST

This magnificent beachfront inn offers guests panoramic views and luxury oceanfront suites. Each of the inn's six airy and spacious guest rooms comes with a sweeping view of the ocean and surrounding beach. Guests will find their rooms stocked with plush robes, a daily supply of complimentary beverages and snacks, and deluxe bath items for a relaxing evening in. In the morning ask for one of the complimentary bicycles or a beach chair and towel.

Let the Beach Bed & Breakfast innkeeper and his staff help you plan the perfect island getaway, just ask about some of the activities around St. Simons Island and they'll help you to coordinate dinner reservations, tee times, and even deep sea fishing excursions. Beach Bed & Breakfast also offers guests luxury spa services that can be enjoyed in the privacy of your own suite.

INNKEEPERS: Joe McDonough & Tomee Sellars

ADDRESS: 907 Beachview Drive, St. Simons Island, Georgia 31522

TELEPHONE: (912) 634-2800; (877) 634-2800

E-MAIL: reserve@beachbedandbreakfast.com

WEBSITE: www.beachbedandbreakfast.com

ROOMS: 6 Suites; Private baths

CHILDREN: Children age 12 and older welcome

PETS: Small pets welcome

Honey-Baked
Croissant Casserole

Makes 10 Servings

"Plan ahead, this dish needs to be prepared the night before."

—INNKEEPER, *Beach Bed & Breakfast*

6 large white, wheat, or butter croissants
1½ cups honey-baked ham, cubed
1 cup cream cheese
½ cup heavy cream
⅛ cup honey
10 large eggs
¼ cup brown sugar
1 cup shredded Swiss cheese

Lightly spray a 9x13x2-inch baking dish with cooking spray. Break up the croissants into small pieces and layer along the bottom of the baking dish. Top with the cubed ham. Using an electric mixer, beat cream cheese, heavy cream, and honey in a large bowl until mixture is smooth. In a separate bowl, scramble the eggs. Pour the cheese and egg mixtures over the ham. Sprinkle the brown sugar and then the Swiss cheese over the top of the casserole, cover, and refrigerate overnight.

The following morning: Preheat oven to 350°F. Bake 30–35 minutes, until top is slightly golden brown.

THE HEARTHSTONE LODGE

I f you're looking for a quiet place to relax and get away from it all, The Hearthstone Lodge is the place for you. This intimate mountain retreat has only three guest rooms which means that you'll always feel comfortable and at home – like you're part of the family. The rustic lodge features warm and welcoming décor, a combination of antiques and traditional handcrafted furnishings. There are five working fireplaces spread throughout the inn, a Jacuzzi and steam room, library and reading area, and a game room with pool table, darts, and a bar. The inn also has a private spa room with massage and aromatherapy.

A stay at the Hearthstone lodge includes Pat's magnificent home-made breakfasts, which are rumored to be so hearty that you won't need to eat again until dinner! Coffee, tea, and afternoon snacks are available daily. Wine and cheese, picnic baskets, champagne, and chocolate covered strawberries are also available, by request and for a little extra, to help make your stay a memorable and romantic one.

INNKEEPERS: Pat & Phil Cunniffe

ADDRESS: 2755 Highway 282, Chatsworth, Georgia 30705

TELEPHONE: (706) 695-0920; (800) 695-0905

E-MAIL: hearthstonelodge@alltel.net

WEBSITE: www.thehearthstonelodge.com

ROOMS: 3 Suites; Private baths

CHILDREN: Cannot accommodate

PETS: Not allowed; Resident pet

Swiss Ham Breakfast Strata

Makes 6 Servings

"Recipe adapted from The Atlantic Journal Constitution.
*Plan ahead, you will need to prepare this up to 3 hours
ahead of time, or overnight."*
—INNKEEPER, *Hearthstone Lodge*

8 ounces diced ham
⅓ cup chopped onion
6 ounces fresh asparagus (cut into ½-inch pieces)
6 cups cubed French or Italian bread, divided
1 tablespoon finely chopped fresh thyme, divided
4 eggs
2½ cups low-fat milk
Salt and pepper to taste
¾ cup grated Swiss or Gruyère cheese

Lightly coat a 2-quart covered baking dish with non-stick cooking spray; set aside. Lightly coat a frying pan with non-stick spray. Cook ham and onion over medium heat until ham is lightly browned and onion is translucent (about 8 minutes). Transfer to a small dish and set aside. In the same skillet, sauté the asparagus until bright green and crisp-tender (about 5 minutes). Cover the bottom of the baking dish with ⅓ of the bread cubes. Add half of the asparagus and about 1 teaspoon of the thyme. Top with another cup of the bread cubes. Top with ham mixture and another teaspoon of thyme. Top with another 1½ cups of the bread and remaining asparagus and thyme. Add in remaining bread cubes.

In a medium bowl, whisk together the eggs and milk until blended. Season with salt and pepper and slowly pour over the casserole taking care to wet each bread cube on the top layer. Sprinkle with grated cheese, cover and chill at least 3 hours, or overnight.

Preheat oven to 350°F. Bake casserole, uncovered, for 1 hour, or until top is browned and center is set. Remove from oven and let rest 10 minutes before serving.

Captain's Quarters B&B

After traveling the world, native Southerners Jim and Julie Powell decided to settle down in Georgia and open their own b&b. Their efforts have truly paid off as they have succeeded in providing each and every guest that visits the Captain's Quarters with a warm and welcoming place to relax and enjoy a taste of true Southern hospitality.

"We enjoyed a marvelous, relaxing, and comfortable stay.
We love the history of the inn and the surrounding area. Thank you,
Jim and Julie, for the luxurious hospitality and the opportunity to make
new friends. Your menus and breakfasts were superb, the rooms lovely
and so comfortable. What a delight to wake up each morning between
soft cotton sheets, hearing the occasionally bird chirping outside!
We also appreciated your kind directions to local sights and your
restaurant recommendations. We hope to come again!" —Guest

INNKEEPERS: Jim & Julie Powell
ADDRESS: 13 Barnhardt Circle, Fort Oglethorpe, Georgia 30742
TELEPHONE: (706) 858-0624; (800) 710-6816
E-MAIL: info@cqinn.com
WEBSITE: www.cqinn.com
ROOMS: 9 Rooms; 2 suites; Private & shared baths
CHILDREN: Children age 13 and older welcome
PETS: Not allowed; Resident pet

Chicken Sausage Strata with Spinach & Asiago Cheese

Makes 12 Servings

"This is a popular dish and is good for a crowd. If you can't find chicken-spinach-asiago sausage, substitute plain chicken sausage. Plan ahead, this dish needs to be prepared the night before."

—INNKEEPER, *Captain's Quarters Bed & Breakfast*

6 cups cubed Italian bread, with crusts
1 pound chicken with spinach
    and asiago cheese sausage
1 (6-ounce) package baby spinach
4 tablespoons diced red bell pepper
2 cups shredded Cheddar cheese
2⅔ cups skim milk
1½ cups Egg Beaters
½ teaspoon dry mustard
½ teaspoon onion powder
½ teaspoon white pepper
½ cup grated Asiago cheese
½ cup Panko bread crumbs
Olive oil

Coat a 9x13-inch baking dish with cooking spray. Spread the bread cubes evenly over the bottom of the dish. Remove the sausage from its casings and crumble over the bread. In a hot, dry wok or skillet, barely wilt the spinach; remove to a cutting board and chop finely. Allow to cool. Layer the spinach, bell pepper, and Cheddar cheese evenly over the sausage. In a bowl, whisk together the milk, Egg Beaters, mustard, onion powder, and whit pepper. Pour the milk mixture over the strata, being sure to moisten all of the bread. Cover and refrigerate 8 hours, or overnight.

The following morning: Preheat oven to 350°F and remove the strata from the fridge. In a small bowl, mix the Asiago cheese and bread crumbs with a little olive oil and sprinkle over the top of the strata. Bake, uncovered, for 30–45 minutes, until the cheeses are melted and the strata is bubbling around the edges.

Green Palm Inn

Green Palm Inn, a folk Victorian "gingerbread classic," is located in the heart of Savannah's famed Historic District. Nestled in a quiet residential neighborhood, just steps away from Greene Square, sits this historic circa 1897 home. Fully renovated and transformed in 1998, the inn now contains four luxury guest rooms each with a king or queen poster or sleigh bed, private bath, and even some working fireplaces. British-Colonial furnishings throughout the inn lend and elegant air and reflect Savannah's British roots.

"The Green Palm Inn is a small, intimate escape on the edge of Savannah's Historic District. Innkeeper Diane is part of what makes this place so special – she prepares exceptional, generous gourmet breakfast, always has sweets available in the afternoon and evening, and serves complimentary wine and cheese every afternoon. She is cordial and welcoming and runs a first-class place. The inn is immaculate, the public areas lovely, and our room met the highest standards…Yes, it is a bit off the beaten track, but it is within a few minutes' leisurely walk to the rest of the District and the Riverfront. A marvelous inn with a wonderful hostess!" —GUEST

INNKEEPER: Diane McCray

ADDRESS: 548 East President Street, Savannah, Georgia 31401

TELEPHONE: (912) 447-8901; (888) 606-9510

E-MAIL: greenpalminn@aol.com

WEBSITE: www.greenpalminn.com

ROOMS: 4 Rooms; 1 Cottage; Private baths

CHILDREN: Children age 16 and older welcome

PETS: Not allowed

Southwest Breakfast Strata

Makes 8 Servings

8 flour tortillas
1 pound pork sausage
¼ cup green peppers, chopped
¼ cup onion, chopped
2 (10-ounce) cans (1 regular and 1 mild)
    tomatoes with green chilies, drained
4 cups shredded sharp Cheddar cheese
6 eggs, beaten
2 cups milk
Salt and pepper, to taste

Spray a 9x13-inch pan with non-stick cooking spray. Tear tortillas into pieces and layer half of the tortillas into the bottom of the pan. In a medium skillet, over medium-high heat, sauté the sausage, peppers, and onion until the sausage is almost cooked through. Add the two cans of drained tomatoes and simmer for 10 minutes. Layer half of the cooked pork mixture over the tortillas. Layer 2 cups of the cheese over the pork. Repeat layers. In a medium bowl, beat together eggs and milk; add salt and pepper. Pour egg mixture over layers; cover pan with foil and refrigerate overnight.

The following morning: Preheat oven to 350°F. Bake 1½ hours, removing foil for final 15 minutes of bake time. Remove from oven and allow to sit 5–10 minutes before serving.

Hamilton-Turner Inn

The magnificent Hamilton-Turner Inn, a lovingly restored Second Empire mansion situated on Lafayette Square in the center of Savannah's historic district, combines gracious hospitality and first class amenities with Southern charm and history. This romantic and elegant inn pampers guests with its personalized service and comforting atmosphere.

Each of the inn's seventeen luxury guestrooms comes with monogrammed robes and spa accessories, quality linens, and stately décor. Many of the rooms have a whirlpool spa bath or claw-foot soaking tubs, fireplaces, and elegant seating areas overlooking the square. The cozy accommodations and welcoming ambiance will make you feel right at home and you may find that you never want to leave.

INNKEEPERS: Jim & Gay Dunlop

ADDRESS: 330 Abercorn Street, Lafayette Square, Savannah, Ga. 31401

TELEPHONE: (912) 233-1833; (888) 448-8849

E-MAIL: innkeeper@hamilton-turnerinn.com

WEBSITE: www.hamilton-turnerinn.com

ROOMS: 11 Rooms; 6 Suites; 1 Carriage house; Private baths

CHILDREN: Children age 12 and older welcome

PETS: Not allowed

Breakfast Vegetable Frittata

Makes 12 Servings

"Plan ahead, this dish will need to be prepared the evening before."

—INNKEEPER, *Hamilton-Turner Inn*

1 red bell pepper	12 eggs
1 yellow bell pepper	3 cups half & half
1 green bell pepper	
1 summer squash	DILL SAUCE
1 zucchini	1 (8-ounce) package
1 stick butter	cream cheese
Mrs. Dash seasoning	1 tablespoon Dijon mustard
Salad croutons, brand	Half & half, as needed
and flavor of choice	to thin sauce
Grated Cheddar cheese	2 tablespoons dill

Dice the peppers and the squash, sauté in butter with generous amounts of Mrs. Dash. Spray a 9x13-inch glass dish with non-stick cooking spray and line the bottom with the croutons. Top with the sautéed vegetables and a layer of Cheddar cheese; use enough cheese to cover the vegetables well. In a medium bowl, beat together the eggs and half & half; slowly pour the mixture over the vegetables. Refrigerate overnight.

The following morning: Preheat oven to 350°F. Bake frittata 1 hour, or until center is cooked through. Cut into 12 squares and then cut each square across the diagonal. Serve two diagonals on a bed of herb cheese grits* and top with dill sauce.

For the sauce: While the dish is baking, combine sauce ingredients and heat in a small saucepan – add just enough half & half to give the sauce the consistency you want.

*For Grits recipe see page 147.

THE DODGE HILL INN

Small towns offer visitors something you just can't get in the big city. The peaceful and serene atmosphere at the Dodge Hill Inn is just that – something you can't get in a big city or a big hotel. Each morning, you'll dine on country ham and local sausage made right in Dodge County. You'll visit with local merchants and other local folk who stop by just to pass the time and swap stories.

Innkeepers Amy, Don, and Helen will be sure to help you find whatever is you need whether it be horseback riding, golf, or a long walk in the country. The welcoming and cheerful ambiance of the Dodge Hill Inn keeps guests coming back again and again.

INNKEEPERS:	Ann & Don Dobbs & Helen Peterson
ADDRESS:	5021 Ninth Avenue, Eastman, Georgia 31023
TELEPHONE:	(478) 374-2644
E-MAIL:	missann@dodgehillinn.com
WEBSITE:	www.dodgehillinn.com
ROOMS:	2 Rooms; 2 Suites; 3 Cottages; Private baths
CHILDREN:	Welcome
PETS:	Not allowed

Tomato & Basil Frittata

Makes 7 Servings

"This frittata is a delicious alternative to the classic quiche and has less fat. Our guests love it! This recipe can also be found in our own cookbook, A Gracious Plenty.*"*

—INNKEEPER, *Dodge Hill Inn Bed & Breakfast*

8 ounces sharp Cheddar cheese
1 tablespoon flour or ground oatmeal
4 ounces Monterey Jack cheese
6 eggs, beaten
½ cup half & half
1 tablespoon Worcestershire sauce
1 medium tomato, chopped
¼ cup fresh basil or chives

Preheat oven to 350°F. Grate the Cheddar cheese and toss with the flour. Pour into a greased 9-inch pie plate. Sprinkle the Monterey Jack over the top. In a medium mixing bowl, beat the eggs and pour in the half & half. Add the Worcestershire sauce and mix well; pour over the cheese. Sprinkle the chopped tomato and herbs over the egg and refrigerate overnight, if desired. Bake 30–35 minutes, until the center is set.

HENSON COVE PLACE
B&B WITH CABIN

Located on 1.6 acres of lush gardens, bordered by two bubbling creeks, sits the rustic and serene Henson Cove Place. This traditional b&b is a great place to kick back and relax. You won't have to worry about a thing. Owners Mariah and Dave make it a point to provide the best service possible and will make sure your stay is both relaxing and rejuvenating. Each morning, Mariah and Dave have

coffee ready for early risers, a hearty homemade breakfast is served each morning, and complimentary snacks and beverages are provided each afternoon. Weekends, you'll be treated to an early evening happy hour complete with hors d'oeuvres.

While this idyllic setting is perfect for relaxing, there are also plenty of other activities available to guests. Whitewater rafting, river tubing, horseback riding, and leisurely hayrides with custom picnics are also available. Nearby Vogel State Park has swimming, hiking, fishing, and paddle boating. Hiawassee also offers plenty of shopping and dining possibilities and there are three nearby golfing locations.

INNKEEPERS: Mariah & Dave Nugent

ADDRESS: 1137 Car Miles Road, Hiawassee, Georgia 30546

TELEPHONE: (706) 896-6195; (800) 714-5542

E-MAIL: relax@henson-cove-place.com

WEBSITE: www.henson-cove-place.com

ROOMS: 2 Rooms; 2 Suites; 1 Cabin

CHILDREN: Welcome; Call ahead

PETS: Welcome; Call ahead; Resident pet

Autumn Eggs with Potatoes & Sausage

Makes 8 Servings

"This dish is very popular with guests; they frequently ask for the recipe. It's both hearty and healthy, and you won't need to eat lunch! Plan ahead, this dish needs to be prepared the night before."

—INNKEEPER, *Henson Cove Place*

½ medium onion, finely chopped
1 tablespoon butter
3 cups cold, cooked potatoes, cut into small cubes
1 pound cooked breakfast sausage
1 (4 ounce) can diced green chilies, drained well
1–2 cups grated cheddar cheese
12 eggs, lightly beaten
¼ teaspoon pepper
Pinch of nutmeg

In a medium saucepan, brown the onion and sausage in a bit of butter. Mix all ingredients together in a large bowl and pour into a greased 9x13-inch pan. Cover and refrigerate overnight.

The following morning: Preheat oven to 350°F. Remove the casserole from the refrigerator and bake 1 hour, or until set. Serve with salsa and garnish with fresh cilantro and chopped tomatoes.

You can halve the recipe and bake in a square 8x8-inch or 9x9-inch pan to serve 4.

Mountain Laurel Creek Inn & Spa

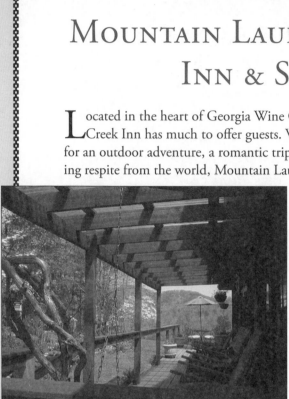

Located in the heart of Georgia Wine Country, Mountain Laurel Creek Inn has much to offer guests. Whether you are looking for an outdoor adventure, a romantic trip for two, or a rejuvenating respite from the world, Mountain Laurel Creek in Dahlonega, Georgia is the place to stay.

For the nature lovers and adventurers among you, canoeing, kayaking, and tubing down the nearby Chestatee and Etowah rivers are great options. If it's just you and your loved one, you can take in a show at the historic Holly Theater, pick up some sweet treats at the Dahlonega Fudge Factory, enjoy a couples massage at the Oasis Day Spa, or take a tour of one of the many local wineries. And if you're just looking to get away from it all and relax, treat yourself to a spa day, visit the Kangaroo Conservation Center, and enjoy a leisure horseback ride.

INNKEEPERS: Dennis Hoover & David Mulcahy
ADDRESS: 202 Talmer Grizzle Road, Dahlonega, Georgia 30533
TELEPHONE: (706) 867-8134
E-MAIL: info@mountainlaurelcreek.com
WEBSITE: www.mountainlaurelcreek.com
ROOMS: 5 Suites; Private baths
CHILDREN: Cannot accommodate
PETS: Not allowed

Breakfast Pot Pie

Makes 2 Servings

*"I wanted to create a recipe that had everything in one dish
and could be made the night before."*

— INNKEEPER, *Mountain Laurel Creek Inn & Spa*

16 frozen tater tots
5 eggs
½ cup half & half
Salt and pepper
2 sausage patties
½ cup broccoli or sliced zucchini
¼ cup shredded Cheddar cheese
4 Pillsbury crescent rolls (1 4 ounce package)

Preheat oven to 350°F. Spray two ramekins with non-stick cooking
spray. Place 8 tater tots in the bottom of each ramekin and place
in the microwave to defrost. Smash the tater tots to make a crust.
In a medium bowl, mix together the eggs and half & half. Add
salt and pepper to taste. Divide the egg mixture evenly between
the two ramekins. Break up the sausage patties and place even
amounts of sausage and broccoli into each ramekin. Sprinkle the
cheese equally over the tops. Roll out the crescent roll dough and
divide into two – each piece will be a square. Cover each ramekin
like a piecrust and bake 1 hour.

The Lodge on Apple Pie Ridge

Indulge yourself with a romantic mountain getaway. This rustic mountain lodge was built over the course of two years using centuries-old pine logs, reclaimed wood, and local stone that give

the inn a charm all its own. The elegant and relaxing setting offers panoramic views of the mountains and surrounding forest. Nature inspired furnishings and artwork are featured throughout the lodge creating a truly warm and inviting atmosphere.

Each guest is treated like one of the family with snacks upon arrival, evening coffee and dessert, and a hearty, multi-course breakfast each morning featuring seasonal specialties and the inn's signature buttermilk biscuits. Attractions located nearby include an 18-hole golf course, whitewater rafting, world-class fishing, and hiking. If you're looking for something more leisure to do with your time, the area also offers excellent local dining, shopping, antiquing, and wineries, as well as year-round farmers' markets and a wide array of seasonal festivals.

INNKEEPERS: Judy & Max Chosewood

ADDRESS: 2154 Apple Pie Ridge Road, Alto, Georgia 30510

TELEPHONE: (706) 776-6012; (888) 339-1374

E-MAIL: lodgeonapplepieridge@alltel.net

WEBSITE: http://lodgeonapplepieridge.com

ROOMS: 5 Rooms; Private baths

CHILDREN: Welcome

PETS: Not allowed

Broccoli Ham Quiche

Makes 6 Servings

"Our son, Casey, experimented and came up with this recipe.
It has been a 'hit' with the guests."

—INNKEEPER, *The Lodge on Apple Pie Ridge*

1 Pillsbury pie crust
Slices of smoked Gouda cheese
⅓ stick margarine
½ cup chopped onion
1 cup chopped broccoli
1 cup chopped ham
5 eggs
¼ cup sour cream
¾ cup half & half
¼ teaspoon salt
¼ teaspoon pepper
1 teaspoon parsley flakes
Shredded cheese

Preheat oven to 375°F. Place the prepared crust in a pie plate; layer the sliced Gouda over the bottom of the crust. In a large skillet over medium-high heat, melt the butter and sauté the broccoli, onion, and ham until the onions are clear. Pour the sautéed mixture over the Gouda cheese. In a small bowl, beat together the eggs, sour cream, and half & half; add salt, pepper, and parsley. Pour the egg mixture over the broccoli mixture. Sprinkle shredded sharp Cheddar cheese over the top of the quiche. Bake 20–30 minutes until lightly browned. Cool 5–10 minutes then serve.

BLUE HERON INN

Located at the edge of a large marsh and a tidal creek, Blue Heron Inn is perfectly situated for bird watching. This nature lovers' retreat features enough porches and balconies to offer an almost 360 degree view of the lush surroundings.

Each of the inn's four rooms is decorated on a different theme. The aptly titled Blue Room, features nautical décor and can be rented as a suite with a private kitchenette while the spacious Blue Heron Room opens up to its own private balcony overlooking the marsh.

Breakfast and the Blue Heron is a real treat that features delectable guest favorites like Lime French Toast and Bill's Shrimp Omelets – made with sweet Georgia Shrimp, of course!

INNKEEPERS: Bill & Jane Chamberlain

ADDRESS: 1 Blue Heron Lane, Darien, Georgia 31319

TELEPHONE: (912) 437-4304

E-MAIL: blueheroninn@darientel.net

WEBSITE: www.blueheroninngacoast.com

ROOMS: 4 Rooms; 2 Suites; Private baths

CHILDREN: Welcome

PETS: Call ahead; Resident pets

Shrimp Omelets

Makes 2 Servings

"This started as a way to use leftover shrimp from the previous night's 'low-country boil' and has become the most requested breakfast on our menu. Goes great with creamy grits and homemade biscuits with jelly."

—INNKEEPER, *Blue Heron Inn*

2 tablespoons vegetable oil
½ cup chopped onions
½ cup chopped green peppers
½ cup chopped mushrooms
¼ cup chopped tomatoes
   (Roma tomatoes work best)
1 dozen shrimp (small to medium shrimp)
   peeled, deveined, and chopped
2 teaspoons Old Bay seasoning
4 eggs
⅓ cup shredded Cheddar cheese
2 sprigs parsley

In a small sauté pan, add enough oil to barely cover the bottom of the pan. Heat oil and add vegetables. Sauté until onions are translucent. Add shrimp and Old Bay seasoning; sauté until shrimp are pink. Pour a small amount of oil into an omelet pan and heat. Beat together two eggs and pour into omelet pan. Cook about 1 minute then add about half of the vegetable and shrimp mixture. Sprinkle with cheese and continue cooking until eggs are cooked to desired consistency. Fold eggs over and slide onto a plate. Repeat the process with remaining eggs and sautéed vegetables and shrimp. Garnish with parsley and serve.

THE BRADY INN

Whether your interests are football, golf, historic homes, or a leisurely weekend browsing for antiques, the Brady Inn B&B is ready to pamper you in classic southern comfort. The Brady Inn is made up of two Victorian era homes, each lovingly restored to their original grace and splendor. Heart pine floors, Victorian mantels, and period décor are featured throughout the inn.

The home-away-from-home atmosphere will make even the weariest traveler feel welcome and relaxed. The inn even offers up its expansive lawns and covered porches for your special event, whether is be a family reunion, or an intimate dinner for two.

INNKEEPERS:	Karen & Peter Wibell
ADDRESS:	250 North Second Street. Madison, Georgia 30650
TELEPHONE:	(706) 342-4400
E-MAIL:	host@bradyinn.com
WEBSITE:	www.bradyinn.com
ROOMS:	7 Rooms; Private baths
CHILDREN:	Welcome
PETS:	Not allowed

The Brady Inn Omelet

Makes 1 Omelet

"Guests love omelets, especially when prepared individually."

—INNKEEPER, *The Brady Inn*

2 ounces white mushrooms
2 green onions
2 ounces cooked ham, sliced
2 tablespoons butter, divided
3 large eggs
1 tablespoon milk
¼ teaspoon salt (optional)
$^{1}/_{8}$ teaspoon pepper (optional)
2 ounces grated Gruyère cheese
Chopped Italian parsley (optional)

Thinly slice the mushrooms and green onions and dice the ham. Sauté in a skillet with 1 tablespoon of butter for approximately 3–5 minutes. While these are sautéing, whisk the eggs in a small bowl; add the milk, salt, and pepper and mix to combine. Heat with the remaining 1 tablespoon of butter in a nonstick 8-inch omelet pan over medium-high heat. Pour the eggs into the pan and cook just until they begin to set. Scramble the eggs using a heat proof rubber spatula. When the eggs begin to form soft, moist curds, spread them into an even layer. Sprinkle the cheese, vegetables, and ham evenly down the center of the omelet. Continue cooking without stirring for another minute, until the omelet is set.

Place the edge of the omelet pan on a work surface next to the serving plate. Tilt the pan while using the spatula to lift one side of the omelet and fold into a half-circle shape. Slide folded omelet onto the plate and brush the top with remaining butter from the mushroom pan. Sprinkle with Italian parsley; serve with fresh fruit and whole grain bread.

Ashford Manor
Bed & Breakfast

A gourmet breakfast with an ever-changing menu is included with your stay at the Ashford Manor. Many of the inn's dishes are prepared using herbs, greens, and even edible flowers from the inn's own gardens. Guests have the option of enjoying their breakfast in the inn's elegant dining room, or en-suite. Items like the mouthwatering Crème Brûlée French Toast are perfect for breakfast in bed!

In the afternoon, enjoy a relaxing walk amongst the magnolias, redbuds, and pines that grace the magnificent grounds, or lounge by the pool and enjoy one the inn's signature mint juleps; their own special ingredient transforms this Southern favorite into something truly memorable.

INNKEEPERS: Mario Castro, Jim & Dave Shearon
ADDRESS: 5 Harden Hill Road, Watkinsville, Georgia 30677
TELEPHONE: (706) 769-2633
E-MAIL: ashfordmanor@charter.net
WEBSITE: www.ambedandbreakfast.com
ROOMS: 5 Rooms; 1 Suite; Private baths
CHILDREN: Children age 14 and older welcome
PETS: Dogs allowed

Ashford Manor Herbed Eggs

Makes 2–3 eggs, per person*

1 teaspoon Dry Vermouth, white wine,
   or leftover champagne, per 3 eggs
Salt and pepper, to taste
Chopped fresh parsley

Herbed Butter:
4–6 tablespoons butter
1 teaspoon fresh chopped parsley
3 teaspoons chopped fresh herbs**
Garlic

In a small bowl, whisk together eggs, liquor, salt, and pepper. In a sauté pan over medium-high heat, melt some of the herbed butter. Pour in the egg mixture and sprinkle with parsley. Scramble to desired doneness. We serve these eggs alone or on puff pastry or crescent roll dough that is shaped in cups.

To prepare herbed butter: Chop fresh herbs into the butter. Mince a small clove of garlic and press into the herb/butter mixture. Cook slowly for 5-10 minutes to meld flavors. Remove from heat and store in refrigerator until ready to use.

*All ingredients should be room temperature. You can either leave the eggs out overnight or warm them in a bowl of water before breaking them.

**You can use any combination of fresh herbs with the parsley. Chives, rosemary, oregano, and thyme are some good ones, but rosemary and oregano are too strong to be used together.

Side Dishes & Sauces

Side Dishes & Sauces

"
Eating well

gives a spectacular joy

to life.
"

—ELSA SCHIAPARELLI

Hamilton-Turner Inn

The Hamilton-Turner Inn is a small inn with a big feel. This charming and elegant inn is the place to stay if you are looking for pampered personalized service and true Southern hospitality. Whether your stay is for business or pleasure, the Hamilton-Turner staff is dedicated to making your stay a memorable one. A gourmet Southern breakfast awaits you each morning. Afternoon tea and sweets, early evening wine and hors d'oeuvres, and late evening port can be found daily in the inn's luxurious parlor.

To occupy your days, the inn offers a wide array of special packages including the Romantic Package which includes champagne and roses in your suite, a gift certificate for dinner at a local restaurant, and an evening carriage ride. The Historic Package includes a trolley tour through historic Savannah, and the Girlfriends' Getaway Package – perfect for a ladies' weekend away from it all – features High Tea at the famous Savannah Tea Room. Whatever you choose, the Hamilton-Turner will help you to plan the perfect vacation in historic Savannah, Georgia.

INNKEEPERS: Jim & Gay Dunlop
ADDRESS: 330 Abercorn Street, Lafayette Square, Savannah, Ga. 31401
TELEPHONE: (912) 233-1833; (888) 448-8849
E-MAIL: innkeeper@hamilton-turnerinn.com
WEBSITE: www.hamilton-turnerinn.com
ROOMS: 11 Rooms; 6 Suites; 1 Carriage house; Private baths
CHILDREN: Children age 12 and older welcome
PETS: Not allowed

HERB CHEESE GRITS

Makes 12 Servings

*"We serve this dish alongside our Breakfast Vegetable Frittata
– see page 129 for recipe."*
—INNKEEPER, *Hamilton-Turner Inn*

4½ cups water
4½ cups half & half
3 cups quick grits (not instant)
Grated cheddar cheese
Chopped parsley
Salt and pepper, to taste

In a large saucepan over medium-high heat, boil water and half
& half. Pour in the grits and cook, stirring constantly, until thickened. Remove from heat and stir in cheese and parsley. Season
with salt and pepper, to taste, and serve with your favorite breakfast dish.

Grits can also be used as a substitute for pasta or rice in many
lunch and dinner entrées.

GLEN-ELLA SPRINGS COUNTRY INN

Glen-Ella Springs Country Inn was constructed as a family home in 1875. The home was eventually expanded to take in paying guests vacationing from coastal Georgia - the mountain location of the inn was a perfect place for a cool summer getaway and respite from the season's plague of yellow fever. Guests took the Tallulah Falls Railroad and were greeted by the inn's owners at the station. Visitors would be transported by horse-drawn buggy or wagon to the inn where they would partake in the healing powers of the inn's fresh mountain spring.

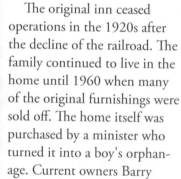

The original inn ceased operations in the 1920s after the decline of the railroad. The family continued to live in the home until 1960 when many of the original furnishings were sold off. The home itself was purchased by a minister who turned it into a boy's orphanage. Current owners Barry and Bobby Aycock purchased the home in 1986 after it had passed through many different hands. After painstaking and loving renovations, the Aycock's reopened the inn. Glen-Ella just celebrated its 20th anniversary in July of 2007!

INNKEEPERS:	Barrie & Bobby Aycock
ADDRESS:	1789 Bear Gap Road, Clarkesville, Georgia 30523
TELEPHONE:	(706 754-7295; (888) 455-8786
E-MAIL:	meetings@glenella.com
WEBSITE:	www.glenella.com
ROOMS:	12 Rooms; 4 Suites; Private baths
CHILDREN:	Welcome
PETS:	Not allowed

Tomato Basil Cheese Grits

Makes 4–6 Servings

*"This recipe was created for our annual Heirloom Tomato Festival
which is held each year in late July. One of our festival events
is a casual Twilight Tomato Supper on our pavilion.
We serve the Tomato Basil Cheese Grits with a braised pork roast
and smoked tomato gravy. For more information about the festival,
got to www.glenella.com."*

—INNKEEPER, *Glen-Ella Springs Country Inn*

2 cups water
1 cup half & half
¾ teaspoon salt
1 cup quick grits, not instant
1 large ripe summer tomato
    (heirloom variety if available), diced
¼ cup fresh basil, finely chopped
2 cups smoked Gouda cheese, shredded
1–2 eggs, beaten
Salt and pepper, to taste as needed

Preheat oven to 400°F. Bring water and half & half to a boil and
add salt. Whisk in the grits and cook, stirring, until thickened
(about 5 minutes). Remove from heat and stir in diced tomato,
basil, and cheese. Taste and adjust seasoning as needed. Whisk in
the eggs.

Pour mixture into a 1½-quart baking dish and bake until firm
and browned on top, 20–30 minutes. Serve immediately.

Fairview Inn B&B

Built in 1895, and located in the heart of Valdosta's oldest residential neighborhoods is the elegant and stately Fairview Inn. Current owners Linda and Irvin Green purchased the home from the original owner's grandson, which makes them only the second family to own the home since the 1800s, a point that they take great pride in. The Green's have made an impressive effort

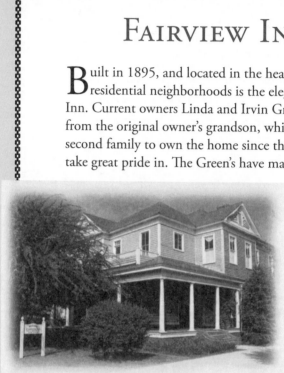

to preserve the original old-South charm and hospitality of the home. Each of the five distinct guest rooms is outfitted to represent the warmth and comfort one would expect in an historic Georgia bed & breakfast.

Just a short walk away, visitors will find historic downtown Valdosta and its many attractions. Begin the day with a hearty breakfast courtesy of the inn and then set off into town to see the sights. Enjoy the historic architecture of the town's beautifully restored courthouse, visit the Lowndes County Historical Society and Museum, take in a performance at the Valdosta Theater Guild, and dine at one the town's quaint local restaurants before returning to the inn to wind down for the evening.

INNKEEPERS: Linda & Irvin Green

ADDRESS: 416 River Street, Valdosta, Georgia 31601

TELEPHONE: (229) 244-6456

E-MAIL: mystay@fairviewinn.info

WEBSITE: www.fairviewinn.info

ROOMS: 4 Rooms; 1 Suite; Private baths

CHILDREN: Welcome

PETS: Not allowed

Tomato Grits

Makes 8–10 Servings

*"People who don't like grits love this dish and
often ask for the recipe. This is a great dish to prepare
the night before and bake the following morning."*
—INNKEEPER, *Fairview Inn Bed & Breakfast*

2 cups water
1¼ cups milk
1 teaspoon salt
1 cup quick grits
1 stick butter
1 (6-ounce) Kraft garlic cheese roll
2½ cups shredded Cheddar cheese
1 (10-ounce) can mild Ro-Tel tomatoes
   and green chilies
2 eggs, slightly beaten

Preheat oven to 350°F. In a saucepan over medium-high heat,
bring the water and half & half to a boil; add the salt. Slowly add
the grits and return mixture to a boil. Stir 1 minute, cover, reduce
heat and cook for 3 minutes. Stir in the butter until it has completely melted; cover and cook an additional 3–5 minutes, until
grits are thick and creamy. Remove from heat and stir in the garlic
cheese and 1½ cups cheddar cheeses. Once the cheese has melted,
add the Ro-Tel tomatoes, mix well and then add the beaten eggs.

Pour the grits into a greased 8x11-inch casserole dish and bake
40 minutes Sprinkle the remaining cheese over the top for the last
5 minutes of cook time.

Roussell's Garden B&B

If you seek true Southern hospitality, and elegant lodgings, Roussell's Garden is the b&b for you. Located in the heart of historic downtown Savannah, the home is a wonderful reminder of a simple and graceful past. Each of the inn's three guest rooms feature four-poster beds outfitted with luxury linens and romantic canopies. The Mandeville Room, the luxurious suite, has huge bay windows and its own private bath complete with a classic claw-foot tub.

Of course, a hearty Southern breakfast served in the dining room or courtyard is included with your stay. Chicken, eggs, biscuits, fresh fruit, coffee, tea, and Janet's famous scalloped hash browns are just a few items you may see on your table. Afternoon tea and wine with assorted cheeses are also served daily.

INNKEEPERS:	Bryan & Janet Roussell
ADDRESS:	208 East Henry Street, Savannah, Georgia 31401
TELEPHONE:	(912) 239-1415
E-MAIL:	info@roussellsgarden.com
WEBSITE:	www.roussellsgarden.com
ROOMS:	3 Rooms; Private & shared baths
CHILDREN:	Cannot accommodate
PETS:	Not allowed

Scalloped Hash Browns

Makes 6 Servings

*"This recipe can be made the night before and baked in the morning.
It is truly a make ahead, quick and tasty recipe."*

—INNKEEPER, *Roussell's Garden Bed & Breakfast*

1 box instant hash brown potatoes
1 can cheddar cheese soup
¼ cup chopped green bell pepper
½ cup crushed corn flakes
3–4 tablespoons olive oil or melted butter
Salt and pepper to taste

Preheat oven to 350°F. Place the instant potatoes in warm water
for approximately 3 minutes and then drain. In a small saucepan,
heat the cheddar cheese soup, 1 can of water, and the green bell
pepper. Add salt and pepper to taste. Mix the cheese sauce with
the hash browns and place in a 13x9-inch sprayed pan. Sprinkle
with crushed corn flakes and drizzle with olive oil or butter. Bake,
uncovered, for about 45 minutes.

White House Farm B&B

While the White House Farm is a great place to relax, there are plenty of things to do and see in Montezuma, Georgia. Visit the nearby Mennonite Restaurant, Bakery and Gift Shop, Kauffman's Farm Market, and the National P.O.W. museum. Also located nearby is the Andersonville Civil War Town. After and afternoon seeing the sites, return to the inn for a quiet afternoon basking in the charm and solitude of the White House Farm.

"...This is an authentic b&b - the family lives downstairs and the rooms to let are on the second floor. There are three bedrooms, each with a bathroom...a breakfast room, and sun porch with separate entrances... The breakfast was homemade and set out, buffet-style, at the time of our choosing...We are city folk and this was a real treat for all of us. The farm is located outside of town, so there is no commercial business within walking distance. I would stay there again; it is a nice place to get away from it all." —GUEST

INNKEEPERS: Crist & Edna Yoder

ADDRESS: 1679 Mennonite Church Road, Montezuma, Ga 31063

TELEPHONE: (478) 472-7942

E-MAIL: home@whitehousefarmbnb.com

WEBSITE: www.whitehousefarmbnb.com

ROOMS: 3 Rooms; Private baths

CHILDREN: Welcome

PETS: Not allowed

Sausage Hash Brown Bake

Makes 12–15 servings

*"This recipe was adapted from one
found in* Taste of Home *magazine."*
—INNKEEPER, *Whitehouse Farm Bed & Breakfast*

2 pounds sausage
2 cups shredded Cheddar cheese
1 (10¾-ounce) can cream of chicken soup
1 cup sour cream
8 ounces French onion dip
1 tablespoon diced onion
¼ cup diced green bell pepper
6–8 cups cooked, shredded potatoes

Preheat oven to 350°F. Fry the sausage in a medium skillet over medium-high heat; set aside. In a medium bowl, mix half of the cheese with soup, sour cream, dip, onion, bell pepper, and potato. Place half of the mixture in the bottom of a greased 9x13-inch pan. Layer the sausage over the potato mixture and top with the remaining potatoes. Sprinkle with the remaining cheese, cover and bake 45–50 minutes. Uncover for the last 10 minutes.

Whitaker-Huntingdon Inn

Whitaker-Huntingdon Inn began life as a private residence in 1883. Previous owners include Murray McGregor Stewart, Savannah's mayor from 1920 to 1924, and Dr. Lloyd Taylor who made many of the current additions so that he could accommodate his medical practice and his growing children. Current owners, Bill and Debbie Saxman, purchased the home in 1976 and opened their b&b in 1995.

With its authentic historic air, magnificent view of Savannah's 32-acre Forsyth Park, and great location, Whitaker-Huntingdon is a great place to stay for your next trip to Savannah.

"My first trip to Savannah was just wonderful....the Whitaker-Huntingdon Inn was a real find for me. Just off Forsyth Park, one mile from the riverfront, the location could not have been better. The walks around Savannah were always just great. Bill and Debbie were wonderful hosts. Bill actually drove me to Bonaventure Cemetery and gave me a tour of the famous cemetery where Johnny Mercer is buried. He went above and beyond... I really loved the charm and hospitality of Bill and Debbie's inn... I'm going back with friends next year. Great find." —Guest

INNKEEPERS:	Bill & Debbie Saxman
ADDRESS:	6002 Whitaker Street, Savannah, Georgia 31401
TELEPHONE:	(912) 232-8911; (877) 232-8911
E-MAIL:	whinn@aol.com
WEBSITE:	www.whinn.com
ROOMS:	4 Rooms; 2 Suites; Private baths
CHILDREN:	Welcome
PETS:	Not allowed; Resident pets

Debbie's Breakfast Sausage Casserole

Makes 4–6 Servings

"We have occasionally used this recipe to encourage neighbors, friends, and city staff to assist in decorating Forsyth Park for the Christmas holidays. During years when this breakfast treat is not offered, volunteers are so small in number that it takes days to finish the decorations. The last year breakfast was provided by the inn as an incentive, over 25 volunteers helped complete the task in about 2 hours!"

—INNKEEPER, *Whitaker-Huntingdon Inn*

1 (1.5-ounce) package yellow rice mix
1 pound packaged sausage (mild or spicy)
1 medium bell pepper, finely chopped
1 medium onion, chopped
1 small can sliced mushrooms, drained
1 can cream of mushroom soup
Dash Worcestershire sauce

Cook the rice per package directions; set aside.

Preheat oven to 350°F. Crumble the sausage into a medium skillet over medium-high heat. Lightly brown the meat with the chopped bell pepper and onion. In a large bowl, combine the rice, sausage mixture, mushrooms, soup, and Worcestershire sauce. Pour into a casserole dish and lightly sprinkle with Cheddar cheese (optional). Bake 30 minutes, or until a bubbly, brown crust forms on top.

We serve this hot and easy breakfast dish with country ham, biscuits and white gravy, and eggs in the cooler months. In warmer months we serve it with fruit.

Garden Walk Inn

Located atop Lookout Mountain, and nestled amongst 100-year-old pines, lies the elegant and peaceful Garden Walk Inn. Each of the inn's cozy rooms and suites is located in one of the ground's private cottages and overlooks the luscious gardens. Covered porches, open decks, and shady balconies are the perfect places to relax with friends and family and enjoy the serene setting.

Each morning, a hearty breakfast is served in the inn's breakfast room, or, weather permitting, on one of the porches. You can spend your day relaxing by the pool, hanging out in the hot tub, or enjoying the area's many attractions. The inn is conveniently located just minutes from Chattanooga where you'll find everything from antique shopping and fine dining to hang gliding and civil war battlegrounds and museums.

INNKEEPERS: Ed & Erma Caballero

ADDRESS: 1206 Lula Lake Road, Lookout Mountain, Georgia 30750

TELEPHONE: (706) 820-4127; (800) 617-0502

E-MAIL: gardenwalk@gardenwalkinn.com

WEBSITE: www.gardenwalkinn.com

ROOMS: 6 Rooms; 6 Suites; 7 Cottages; Private baths

CHILDREN: Welcome

PETS: Not allowed

Sausage Casserole

Makes 12 Servings

"Guests try to identify this dish by calling it dirty rice,
hash, and wild rice mix, amongst other things."

—INNKEEPER, *Garden Walk Inn*

1 pound sausage
1 pound ground beef
1 small onion
1 (6-ounce) package wild rice
1 (8-ounce) can sliced water chestnuts
4–5 tablespoons soy sauce

In a large skillet over medium-high heat, brown sausage, beef, and onion; set aside. Cook wild rice according to package instructions, omitting butter. In a large bowl, mix together cooked rice with cooked meat mixture. Add water chestnuts and soy sauce to mixture and set aside to cool. Place entire mixture in a crock-pot on low heat until ready to serve.

This mixture can be frozen for future use. Simply heat up in the microwave and place mixture in the crock-pot (set on low) to heat overnight.

GARDEN HOUSE B&B

This quaint and quiet bed & breakfast is a great place for a relaxing weekend away from the hustle and bustle of everyday life. Owners Doug and Rhoda Joyner make it their goal to pamper their guests. The inn offers only one guest suite, the entire top story of the home, providing guests with a truly private and quiet lodging experience. Daily refreshments are provided as is a mouthwatering Southern breakfast catered to your taste.

Garden House is conveniently located just five blocks from the heart of Decatur. A short walk will find you amongst antique and gift shops, as well as local restaurants. Decatur is also located just 6 miles from Atlanta making it a great tourist destination.

INNKEEPERS: Doug & Rhoda Joyner

ADDRESS: 135 Garden Lane, Decatur, Georgia 30030

TELEPHONE: (404) 377-3057

E-MAIL: reservations@gardenhousebedandbreakfastdecatur.com

WEBSITE: http://gardenhousebedandbreakfastdecatur.com

ROOMS: 1 Suite; Private bath

CHILDREN: Welcome

PETS: Not allowed

Sausage & Pan Fried Apples

Makes 6 Servings

"This dish was first prepared by our friend Wesley Kersey.
We like to serve these as a side with eggs or an omelet.
It looks pretty and enticing!"

—INNKEEPER, *Garden House Bed & Breakfast*

1 pound sausage, Polish or Kielbasa style
3 large apples, tart redskins like Winesap work best
½ stick butter
2–3 tablespoons brown sugar
½ teaspoon apple pie mix, or cinnamon

Slice the sausage into ½-inch rounds (thicker is fine if you prefer) and sauté in a dry skillet over high heat until browned. Remove from pan and drain excess grease. Thinly slice the apples and set aside. Melt the butter in the same skillet and add apples. Sauté apples in butter until they are softened but not mushy, add the brown sugar and spice. Return the sausage to the pan and stir together until both apples and sausage are coated with sugar and spice. Remove from heat and serve.

The Woodbridge Inn
Restaurant & Lodge

The elegant Woodbridge Inn Restaurant & Lodge sits on land steeped in history. From the East Dining Room guests can look out upon the majestic Sharptop Mountain, which was once a worship place for the Cherokee Indians. On the Inn's West side is the Old Federal Road, a path used by General Andrew Jackson on his way to Florida, and also used as camping ground for both Union and Confederate soldiers during the Civil war. The building itself began as an inn for travelers in the mid-1800s. Current owners, Joe and Brenda, purchased the inn in 1976 and have been delighting guests ever since.

Today, the inn features 18 luxurious guest rooms and three rental houses for extended stays. The inn's restaurant has an ever-changing selection of mouthwatering daily and seasonal specials such as lobster cakes, roast duck, fresh venison, and even ostrich.

INNKEEPERS: Joe & Brenda Rueffert
ADDRESS: 44 Chambers Street, Jasper, Georgia 31043
TELEPHONE: (706) 253-6293
E-MAIL: woodbridge@woodbridgeinn.net
WEBSITE: www.woodbridgeinn.net
ROOMS: 18 Suites; Private baths
CHILDREN: Welcome
PETS: Welcome; Resident pets

Bavarian Red Cabbage

Makes 6–8 Servings

6 strips applewood smoked bacon
1 sweet yellow onion
1 head red cabbage
½ cup sugar
1 teaspoon salt
2 bay leaves
¼ cup Worcestershire sauce
1 teaspoon allspice
¼ cup tarragon vinegar
2 teaspoons ground cloves
2 tablespoons fresh cracked peppercorns

Place (in order) bacon, onions, and cabbage into the bottom of a heavy bottom pot and cook over low for about 30 minutes. While the cabbage is cooking, mix together the remaining ingredients in a medium mixing bowl. Once the cabbage has reduced, add the sugar mixture to the pot. Stir together and cook another 30 minutes.

Serve fresh or keep in the refrigerator up to 2 days.

Cedar House Inn & Yurts

In the heart of Dahlonega lies a lodging experience like no other. At Cedar House Inn and Yurts guests have the option of staying in one of the inn's cozy indoor pine-walled rooms, or one of two unique yurts. Though the yurts resemble large canvas tents, they each offer all the same luxuries as an indoor room. Queen sized beds, air conditioning/heating (depending on the weather), private bathhouse, floors covered in oriental rugs, and electricity – sleep under the stars with all the comforts of home!

In the morning, enjoy a scrumptious vegetarian breakfast featuring the likes of peaches and cream stuffed French toast with home-made blackberry syrup, fresh corn fritters, fried apples, fresh baked muffins, and mushroom quiche. The dishes vary by season and are all made from fresh and organic ingredients.

INNKEEPERS: Fred & Mary Beth Tanner
ADDRESS: 6463 Highway 19 North, Dahlonega, Georgia 30533
TELEPHONE: (706) 867-9446
E-MAIL: mtnhomeinn@windstream.net
WEBSITE: www.cedarhouseinn.net
ROOMS: 2 Rooms; 1 Suite; 2 Yurts; Private baths
CHILDREN: Cannot accommodate
PETS: Not allowed; Resident pets

Fried Potatoes with Sweets

Makes 4 Servings

"I'm a firm believer in colorful foods for good health and eye appeal. When the local grocer began carrying very small sweet potatoes, it seemed the perfect time to add color and vitamin A to a favorite morning dish."

—INNKEEPER, *Cedar House Inn & Yurts*

2–3 tablespoons olive oil
2 small sweet potatoes, thinly sliced
3 medium white potatoes, thinly sliced
1 medium onion, thinly sliced
Water
Salt and pepper, to taste

Heat a 12-inch skillet over medium heat for approximately 3 minutes. Pour in olive oil to coat pan. Layer the potato slices in the pan with the white potato slices on the bottom – the sweets tend to burn if placed on the bottom. Sprinkle onions over the top. Cover the pan and allow to cook about 10 minutes (sprinkle water over the top of the potatoes at the 5 minute mark to allow steaming and reduce the need for more oil), or until slices at the bottom of the pan are brown on one side. Cook, turning occasionally, until all the potato slices are tender, approximately 5–10 minutes longer. Season with salt and pepper and serve.

Fresh Corn Fritters

Makes 4 Servings

*"These fritters are best at the peak of summer when corn
is sweet and tender. I've included a simple modification
that makes these a real treat for gluten-free guests."*

—Innkeeper, *Cedar House Inn & Yurts*

3 ears fresh corn, kernels and scrapings
2 large eggs
2 tablespoons buttermilk or half & half
1½ tablespoons unsalted butter, melted
1 tablespoon sugar
½ teaspoon salt
Cooking spray
4 tablespoons all-purpose flour*

To cut kernels and scrapings from corn, stand one ear upright in a
shallow pan. Slice down all sides of the ear with a medium knife,
cutting only about half of the kernel away. Next, turn the knife
over and push the dull side of the blade down all sides of the ear.

Place the kernels and scrapings in a medium bowl. Mix in eggs,
milk, and melted butter. Sprinkle in the flour, sugar, salt, and
baking powder, stirring until just combined. Coat a heavy pan
or skillet with cooking spray and heat over medium flame. Spoon
the batter onto the pan (about 2 tablespoons per fritter) and cook
until tiny bubbles form on their tops. Check to be sure they are
done on the bottom and turn carefully – they tear easily.

Top fritters with maple syrup, fruit topping, salsa, red pepper
jelly, fruit chutney, or just powdered sugar.

*To make these gluten-free, use 2 tablespoons buckwheat flour
and 2 tablespoons white rice flour.

Greens with Raspberry Chipotle Sauce

Makes 4 Servings

"I had little experience with cooking fresh greens when I first began preparing this recipe. I couldn't understand why this dish was so gritty when I had so carefully washed my greens before cooking them. Then a helpful guest suggested that I soak them instead, and presto – the problem was gone! Soaking the greens with a little strategic swishing allows the dirt to float off and settle to the bottom of your pan or sink."

—INNKEEPER, *Cedar House Inn & Yurts*

2 tablespoons olive oil
1 cup chopped onion
3 cloves garlic, chopped
4 cups kale, collards, or chard, washed and drained
1–2 tablespoons soy sauce, to taste

Raspberry Chipotle Sauce:
$\frac{1}{3}$ cup raspberry spread or jam
2 teaspoons canned chipotles in adobo sauce
2 tablespoons water
1–3 teaspoons lemon juice

Heat a 12-inch skillet over medium heat for about 3 minutes then coat with olive oil. Sauté the onions until they begin to soften, add garlic and cook one more minute. Add the greens, stirring to mix with the onion and garlic, and cover. Cook, stirring occasionally, until greens begin to wilt. Add soy sauce and continue cooking, covered and still stirring occasionally, until greens are tender. Add additional water to seam if greens become too dry.

For the raspberry chipotle sauce: In a small saucepan, stir raspberry jam, chipotles, and water. Simmer over low heat until hot and saucy. Add 1 teaspoon lemon juice. Add water as needed to thin sauce (if necessary) and more lemon to taste.

Variation: To serve this as a vegan scramble, mash 1 block of firm tofu into 3 tablespoons of soy sauce and mix into greens. No a additional soy sauce is needed for greens if you add this variation.

Beach Bed & Breakfast

Beach Bed & Breakfast is a luxury beach resort found within a cozy bed & breakfast. Voted one of Coastal Living's "top 25 Inns we love," the Beach B&B provides all the comforts of home with quality one-on-one service and a glorious setting. Lounging on the beach is the recommended activity for all vacationers, but you can also see the sites of historic St. Simon's Island. Local attractions include ghost tours, the St. Simon's Lighthouse, carriage rides, pontoon boat tours, and of course, plenty of local shopping and dining.

"…Our room was beautiful, the overall accommodations were great, and the staff top notch. We enjoyed breakfast each morning on a balcony overlooking the ocean, rode bikes around the island… ate at local restaurants (the staff secured out reservations), and lounged on the beach with chairs and beach towels provided by the B&B. I only wish we could have stayed longer before returning to reality!" —GUEST

INNKEEPERS: Joe McDonough & Tomee Sellars
ADDRESS: 907 Beachview Drive, St. Simons Island, Georgia 31522
TELEPHONE: (912) 634-2800; (877) 634-2800
E-MAIL: reserve@beachbedandbreakfast.com
WEBSITE: www.beachbedandbreakfast.com
ROOMS: 6 Suites; Private baths
CHILDREN: Children age 12 and older welcome
PETS: Small pets welcome

Roasted Walnut Quesadilla with Cherry Preserves

Makes 6 Servings

6 (8-inch) flour tortillas
1½ cups shredded Havarti Cheese
12 tablespoons chopped toasted walnuts
1 cup cherry preserves
Vegetable cooking spray
6 fresh cherries or strawberries, for garnish

Sprinkle one side of an 8-inch flour tortilla with ¼ cup shredded Havarti cheese; top with 2 tablespoons chopped, toasted walnuts.

Fold the tortilla over the filling. Coat a non-stick skillet with vegetable cooking spray and cook quesadilla over medium heat – 2 minutes per side, or until cheese is melted. Remove from heat and slice into wedges. Serve with cherry preserves and fresh cherries or strawberries as garnish.

THE FITZPATRICK HOTEL

The Fitzpatrick Hotel first opened its doors to guests in 1900 and has operated as one of Washington's top inns ever since. The inn was fully restored to its natural grace and splendor between 2002 and 2004 and is now listed on the Registry of Historic Places. This small but grand boutique hotel is perfect for a short weekend getaway or a long romantic escapade with that special someone.

"Everything about the Fitzpatrick was outstanding. It was like stepping back in time to a gentler way of life – around the turn of the 20th century. In our room on the third floor, I thought I detected a female presence and smelled a flowery perfume, but nothing scary, and, of course, it could have been my imagination. We met another couple who said they heard the place was haunted by a lady in green, phantom piano music, party sounds near the ballroom, and so on. But the Fitzpatrick is the sort of place that wouldn't be complete without a ghost or two. I highly recommend the Fitzpatrick. You won't be disappointed." —GUEST

INNKEEPERS: Tom Jones

ADDRESS: 16 West Square, Washington, Georgia 30673

TELEPHONE: (706) 678-5900

E-MAIL: info@thefitzpatrickhotel.com

WEBSITE: http://thefitzpatrickhotel.com

ROOMS: 16 Rooms; 1 Suite; Private baths

CHILDREN: Welcome

PETS: Not allowed

Caesar Dressing

Makes 2 1/2 Quarts

"We developed this variation of a the classic Caesar dressing because of the danger in using raw eggs. We make our recipe separately then toss with the greens and croutons, garnishing with extra croutons and cheese."

—INNKEEPER, *The Fitzpatrick Hotel*

1 (14-ounce) can jack mackerel
3 tablespoon olive oil
2 quarts mayonnaise
½ cup vinegar
½ cup grated Parmesan cheese
2 ounces fish sauce
½ ounce Tabasco
½ ounce Worcestershire sauce
1 tablespoon garlic, freshly chopped
½ tablespoon black pepper
1 teaspoon salt
Water, as needed for consistency

In a food processor filled with a stainless steel blade, combine the mackerel (bones and all) and the olive oil to create a wet, fine paste. Transfer to a large mixing bowl. Add mayonnaise, vinegar, Parmesan, fish sauce, Tabasco, Worcestershire, garlic, pepper, salt, and water (as needed) to make a thick mayonnaise with a fishy taste. Adjust with more fish sauce, Parmesan, or any other ingredient to taste.

To make Caesar salad: In a large mixing bowl combine chopped romaine lettuce, grated Parmesan cheese, and croutons. Pour 2 ounces of the dressing along the sides of the bowl and toss to combine. Garnish with extra cheese and croutons to serve.

Appetizers, Soups, & Salads

Appetizers, Soups & Salads

" The real American pattern
of feeding is the snack.
It lasts from early morning

to bedtime. "

—JOHN HESS

THE BEECHWOOD INN

The Beechwood Inn Bed & Breakfast and Wine Cellar is a
California style wine retreat in the heart of Georgia. Owners
David and Gayle Darugh bottle their own wines from Georgia and
Oregon grown grapes. Treat yourself and choose from their 3,000-
bottle wine cellar, which features a selection from all around the
world. Enjoy afternoon tastings, special wine events, and even cooking classes courtesy of the inn.

The inn's restaurant, Winner of the 2007 *Wine Spectator* Award
of Excellence, features California and Mediterranean style meals
using only the best in organic local produce. A weekend Prixe Fixe
menu is available through advance reservation and is the best way to
sample some of the inn's mouthwatering fare.

INNKEEPERS:	David & Gayle Darugh
ADDRESS:	220 Beechwood Drive, Clayton, Georgia 30525
TELEPHONE:	(706) 782-5485 (866) 782-2485
E-MAIL:	david-gayle@beechwoodinn.ws
WEBSITE:	www.beechwoodinn.ws
ROOMS:	2 Rooms; 5 Suites; 1 Cottage; Private baths
CHILDREN:	Children age 12 and older welcome
PETS:	Dogs welcome; Resident pets

Gruyère Cheese Gougères

Makes 4 Dozen

"Gougères are a classical preparation often served at wine tastings in France. The puffs are made from a savory pâte à choux, or cream puff dough. They are best served hot out of the oven. If you eliminate the cheese, the puff can be used as a base for a dessert."

—INNKEEPER, *Beechwood Inn*

1 cup water (or skim milk)
7 tablespoons unsalted butter
1 tablespoon kosher salt, or more to taste
Pinch of sugar
1¼ cups all-purpose flour
4–5 large eggs
1¼ cups grated Gruyère cheese
Freshly ground white pepper

Preheat oven to 450°F and line two baking sheets with Silpats or parchment paper. In a medium saucepan, combine water, butter, salt, and sugar and bring to a boil. Add all of the flour at once and reduce heat to medium. Stir with a wooden spoon for 2 minutes, or until the mixture forms a ball and the excess moisture has evaporated (if the ball forms more quickly, continue to cook and stir for a full 2 minutes). Transfer the mixture to a bowl of a mixer fitted with the paddle and beat for 30 seconds at medium speed to cool – you can do this by hand if your arm is strong. Add the 4 eggs one at a time and continue to mix until completely combined and the batter has a smooth, silky texture. The batter in the mixing bowl should form a peak with a top that falls over. If it is too stiff, beat in the white of the remaining egg. Check again, and add the yolk if necessary. Finally, mix in the cheese and season with salt and pepper.

Using an oiled spoon, drop one tablespoon of dough onto the sheet. Sprinkle the tops with additional cheese and bake 7–8 minutes, or until the puff and hold their shape. Reduce heat to 350°F and bake an additional 20–25 minutes. When they are done, the gougères will be light golden brown on the outside, and hollow, but slightly moist, on the inside. Remove from pan and serve while hot.

Fresh Thai Basil Rolls
with Satay Sauce

Makes 6 Servings

Rolls:
1 package round rice paper wrappers
1 package cellophane noodles
   soaked in hot water 20 minutes
1 can cocktail shrimp, drained,
   or 1 cup small cooked shrimp
½ cup bean sprouts
1 bunch fresh Thai basil
3 tablespoons grated fresh ginger
½ cup fresh cilantro, chopped
3 spring onions, finely chopped
1 ounces pimento strips
3 cups finely shredded
   Rabun County Cabbage
1 tablespoon soy sauce
2 tablespoons rice wine vinegar
3 tablespoons fresh lime juice
½ cup toasted sesame seed oil
Grated rind from 1 lime

Satay Sauce:
1 cup dry-roasted peanuts
⅓ cup water
1 clove garlic, minced
½ teaspoon dark soy sauce
2 teaspoons sesame oil
2 tablespoons brown sugar
2 tablespoons fish sauce
½ teaspoon tamarind paste
1 teaspoon red chili sauce
   (more or less to taste)
Fresh lime juice

For rolls: Toss all roll ingredients, except rice wrappers and Thai basil, together in a bowl. Fill a large bowl with hot water and submerge one rice wrapper around 30 seconds to soften. Remove and place on a clean surface. Soak your second wrapper while filling your first. Place a heaping tablespoon of roll mixture on the rice paper. Leaving a 1-inch border spread the mixture over the wrapper and top with 3 Thai basil leaves. Roll bottom of wrapper halfway up, wrapping tightly. Fold in the sides and continue to roll up. Keep rolls refrigerated until ready to serve.

For satay sauce: In a food processor or blender, mix all sauce ingredients. You may serve this sauce cold or warm, depending on your preference.

Smoked Heirloom Tomato Sauce with Ravioli

Makes 6 Servings

5 pounds sun-ripe heirloom tomatoes
½ cup olive oil
3 tablespoons balsamic vinegar
Salt and pepper
20–30 garlic cloves
3 tablespoons tomato paste
3 fresh sage leaves, sliced into chiffonade
1 teaspoon sugar
2 tablespoons salt
32 ounces fresh (or frozen) cheese filled ravioli
½ cup fresh basil, sliced into chiffonade
Grated rind from 2 lemons
1 cup freshly grated Parmigiano Reggiano

Slice the tomatoes in half (or quarters if they are large). Place them all sliced-side-up in a large bowl or sheet pan. Drizzle olive oil and vinegar over the tomatoes and sprinkle with salt and pepper. Marinate 4 hours then transfer to racks and cold smoke with hickory for 3 hours. Place the garlic in a garlic roaster and roast at 350°F for 45 minutes, shaking every 15 minutes.

Purée the smoked tomatoes, roasted garlic, and tomato paste in a food processor until smooth. Pour into a 3-qaurt pan and cook over medium heat until the sauce is thick (up to 3 hours). Taste for seasoning and add salt to taste as well as about a teaspoon of sugar. Add shredded sage and stir to blend. Boil salted water and add ravioli; cook to al dente. Serve 3 ravioli per appetizer plate. Top with a ladle of sauce, basil chiffonade, lemon rind, and grated cheese.

THE GASTONIAN

The Gastonian is comprised of two adjacent Regency-Italianate mansions built in 1868. This four-diamond, award-winning b&b has even been recognized by *Condé Naste Traveler* Magazine as one of the finest places to stay in world. Known for its intimate atmosphere, authentic antiques, grand décor, and personalized service, the Gastonian provides guests with a truly luxurious vacation experience.

In 2000, the inn was selected for membership in the international association of luxury hotels and restaurants cementing its position as the premiere lodging experience in Savannah, Georgia.

INNKEEPER:	Melanie Bliss
ADDRESS:	220 East Gaston Street, Savannah, Georgia 31401
TELEPHONE:	(912) 232-2869; (800) 322-6603
E-MAIL:	concierge@gastonian.com
WEBSITE:	www.gastonian.com
ROOMS:	15 Rooms; 2 Suites; Private baths
CHILDREN:	Children age 12 and older welcome
PETS:	Not allowed

Vidalia Onion Bites

Makes 6–8 servings

²/₃ cup mayonnaise
²/₃ cup sour cream
1 cup Parmesan cheese
1 cup Vidalia onion, finely chopped
1 loaf sliced sandwich bread

Preheat oven to 350°F. Mix together the mayonnaise, sour cream, Parmesan cheese, and onion. Cut the crusts off of the bread and spread the onion mixture over each slice. Cut into bite-sized pieces and place on a cookie sheet. Bake 10 minutes, or until golden brown. Serve immediately.

You can spice up the spread with cayenne or black pepper, or Italian seasoning.

Twelve hors d'oeuvres per guest is the rule of thumb when it's the only food served at a cocktail party.

Barn Inn at Lake Rabun

The Barn Inn at Lake Rabun began life as a horse stable built in the 1920s for an heir to the Coca-Cola fortune. The inn was purchased in 1954 by Dr. S. R. Love and his wife, Madah, who began using the barn for lodging and spiritual retreats after the doctor's death. Though it was used for lodging, at the time it had not yet been renovated for this purpose. In 1984 the barn was finally converted to a bed & breakfast and has operated as such until 1998 when the owners began using it as their private residence.

Current owners, Jan and Nancy, purchased the inn in 2005 and reopened the bed & breakfast the following year after painstaking renovations. Their efforts have turned the inn into a relaxing and romantic mountain getaway.

INNKEEPERS:	Jan Timms & Nancy Gribble
ADDRESS:	31 Barn Inn Road, Lakemont, Georgia 30552
TELEPHONE:	(706) 212-9995
E-MAIL:	barninnjan@windstream.net
WEBSITE:	www.barninn.com
ROOMS:	6 Rooms; Private baths
CHILDREN:	Children ages 14 and older welcome
PETS:	Not allowed

Cheese Crispies

Makes 60–65 Wafers

½ pound sharp Cheddar cheese
2 sticks margarine
2 cups self-rising flour
½ teaspoon red pepper
Dash of salt
2 cups Rice Krispies

Preheat oven to 350°F. Grate the cheddar cheese into a large bowl and blend with softened margarine. In a small bowl, sift together flour, red pepper, and salt; combine with the cheese mixture. Stir in the Rice Krispies and form the mixture into small balls (about a teaspoon per ball). Place the balls on a cookie sheet and press flat with a fork. Bake 20-25 minutes. Remove from oven and allow to cool on the pan for 5 minutes.

Serve with chutney or hot pepper jelly for topping.

Cheese & Spinach Puffs

Makes about 60 Puffs

1 (10 ounce) package frozen,
    chopped spinach
½ cup chopped onion
2 eggs, slightly beaten
½ cup grated Parmesan cheese
½ cup shredded Cheddar cheese
½ cup blue cheese salad dressing
½ cup melted butter
¼ teaspoon garlic powder
1 cup Bisquick

In a medium saucepan, combine spinach and onion; cook according to spinach package directions. Drain well, pressing out all liquid. In a large bowl, combine eggs, cheeses, salad dressing, butter, and garlic powder. Add the spinach mixture and Bisquick and mix well. Cover and chill until mixture can be shaped into 1-inch balls.* Chill formed balls, covered, until ready to serve.

Preheat oven to 350°F. Place chilled puffs on a baking sheet and bake 10–12 minutes. Serve warm.

*After shaping, the puffs can be frozen. Bake frozen puffs, using same directions above, 12–15 minutes.

Salmon Ball

Makes 1 Ball

"This recipe was adapted from one found in an old
Southern Living *cookbook. Plan ahead, you'll need several hours*
to refrigerate before serving."

—INNKEEPER, *Barn Inn at Lake Rabun*

1 large can salmon
1 (8 ounce) package cream cheese
2 tablespoons freshly squeezed lemon juice
4 green onions, minced
3 tablespoons horseradish
1 teaspoon Worcestershire sauce
Several dashes cayenne pepper, to taste
½ cup chopped pecans
3 tablespoons minced fresh parsley

Drain the salmon and remove any skin or bones; flake meat with a fork. With a mixer, whip the cream cheese; blend in lemon juice, onion, horseradish, Worcestershire, and cayenne pepper. Once the mixture is well blended, stir in the flaked salmon and pecans.

Line a small bowl with plastic wrap and pack mixture in tightly. Cover and chill at least several hours, or overnight. Unmold and roll the ball in the parsley. Serve with your choice of crackers.

1842 Inn

The elegant and stately 1842 Inn, in Macon, Georgia, has made its way into many local and travel magazines including Elegant Southern Culture, Travel, and Macon Style. All of them agree that the 1842 Inn is one of Macon's most luxurious historic inns. Each of the inn's gorgeously appointed guest rooms is named for a different historic Georgia figure and features period antiques. Most of the rooms also include working fireplaces, canopied beds, and whirlpool tubs earning it the coveted AAA Four-Diamond rating as well as a spot on the American Historic Inns Top 10 Most Romantic Inns in America list.

"One look at the 1842 Inn and you'll swear you've stepped back into a scene from 'Gone With the Wind,' where your only concerns for the day are where to sit on the massive verandah and enjoy one of Joanne's special mint juleps or how to balance your time between the beautiful appointed guest rooms and inviting public areas."
—Southern Culture *magazine*

INNKEEPER: Nazario Filipponi
ADDRESS: 353 College Street, Macon, Georgia 31201
TELEPHONE: (877) 452-6599
E-MAIL: management@1842inn.com
WEBSITE: www.1842inn.com
ROOMS: 19 Rooms; Private baths
CHILDREN: Welcome
PETS: Call ahead

1842 Inn's Cheese Straw Daisies

Makes 12 Servings

8 ounces sharp Cheddar cheese, grated
½ cup vegetable shortening
1 stick butter
$^3/_8$ teaspoon cayenne pepper
1 teaspoon water
$^1/_3$ cup grated Parmesan cheese
2 rounded cups all-purpose flour, sifted
1 teaspoon baking powder

Preheat oven to 350°F. In a food processor, blend the cheddar cheese; add the shortening, and butter and continue blending. Add the cayenne pepper and water and pulse to blend. Add the Parmesan cheese and pulse once again. In a small bowl, combine flour and baking powder; add to the cheese mixture ⅓ at a time, pulsing between each addition.

Stuff the dough into a pastry bag fitted with the star tip. Squeeze 70–80 daisies (between 1 and 1½ tablespoons each) onto a large baking sheet. Bake 10–12 minutes. Allow to cool and serve.

109 WEST

This elegantly furnished 1871 Italianate estate home is located in Savannah's landmark historic district. It's the perfect place for wedding parties, family or group vacations, corporate retreats, and other special events. The entire property can accommodate up to 26 guests and features a beautiful courtyard that can be used for social events.

"My husband and I had a wonderful stay in the carriage house! It was absolutely perfect – the location, the décor, the privacy… everything exceeded our expectations. The accommodations were beautiful and elegant, and the location was in the heart of the historic district. All the sights were within pleasant walking distance. We are looking forward to planning another stay at 109 West in the future." —GUEST

INNKEEPER: Robbie Bell
ADDRESS: 109 West Liberty Street, Savannah, Georgia 31401
TELEPHONE: (912) 232-6633
E-MAIL: reservations@broughtonst.com
WEBSITE: www.109west.net
ROOMS: 10 Rooms; Private & shared baths
CHILDREN: Welcome
PETS: Not allowed

Spinach Squares

Makes 10–12 Servings

"We adapted this recipe from one found in the Atlanta Journal Constitution. *This is a very simple recipe to make and uses ingredients that are usually on hand. Very tasty!"*

—INNKEEPER, *109 West*

1 cup all-purpose flour
1 teaspoon salt
1 teaspoon baking powder
2 eggs, beaten
1 cup milk
¼ cup melted butter or margarine
½ cup chopped onion
1 pound shredded cheddar cheese (low-fat)
1 (10-ounce) package frozen chopped spinach,
    thawed and drained or squeezed

Preheat oven to 350°F. In a large bowl, combine flour, salt, and baking powder. Stir in beaten eggs, milk, and butter. Add remaining ingredients and stir until moistened. Pour mixture onto a lightly greased 9x13-inch baking pan. Bake 35 minutes. Remove and allow to cool about 5 minutes before cutting into squares.

Cheese & Spinach Spread

Makes 12 Servings

*"My sister gave us this recipe. It is very easy to make,
can be put together in minutes, and guests seem to love it!"*
—INNKEEPER, *109 West*

4 ounces Velveeta cheese, cubed
4 ounces, sharp Cheddar cheese, shredded
4 ounces Monterey Jack cheese, shredded
1 (10-ounce) package frozen chopped spinach
1 (8-ounce) jar salsa

Preheat oven to 350°F. Place the three cheeses in a microwave-safe container and microwave for 1 minute. Remove and stir. Return to microwave for 1 minute. Squeeze thawed spinach to drain excess water; mix spinach into cheese mixture. Stir in salsa and mix well. Bake 25 minutes in preheated oven.

Serve warm with chips or crackers.

Blue Cheese Pecan Grapes

Makes 12 Servings

"This recipe was adapted from our church cookbook."
—INNKEEPER, *109 West*

    1 (4-ounce) package crumbled blue cheese
    1 (3-ounce) package cream cheese, softened
    30 seedless grapes (green or red)
    1 cup finely chopped pecans

In a small bowl, combine blue and cream cheeses. Beat at medium speed until smooth. Cover and chill mixture at least 1 hour.

Wash and dry grapes; wrap each grape with enough cheese to cover, about 1 teaspoon per grape. Roll cheese covered grapes in pecans; cover and chill 1 hour before serving.

Historic Statesboro Inn & Restaurant

The Statesboro Inn is made up of two turn-of-the-century houses. The Brannen House, a Victorian-style farmhouse was built in 1881 and features four guest rooms. The Raines house, built in 1904 is a combination of Victorian and Neoclassical architecture. Both have been fully renovated and are now on the National Register of Historic Places.

Each of the inn's seventeen guest rooms features a combination of modern conveniences and period décor. Every room is wholly unique – some even have private porches and jetted tubs. There is also a private, two-bedroom cabin on location with its own kitchen and living room, great for traveling families. Of course, a full breakfast comes with your stay. The inn even offers weekday lunches and a traditional home-cooked Southern buffet every Sunday.

INNKEEPER: Denman DuBose

ADDRESS: 106 South Main Street, Statesboro, Georgia 30458

TELEPHONE: (912) 489-8628; (800) 846-9466

E-MAIL: mandyatstatesboroinn@yahoo.com

WEBSITE: www.statesboroinn.com

ROOMS: 17 Rooms; 1 Suite; Private baths

CHILDREN: Welcome

PETS: Welcome; Resident pets

Shrimp Bisque

Makes 12 Servings

½ pound butter
1 large onion, minced
1 large red pepper, puréed
2 cups flour
1 pint heavy cream
½ gallon milk
1½ pounds raw shrimp,
    peeled and deveined
3 cups chicken stock
2 tablespoons tomato paste
1 tablespoon salt
1 tablespoon white pepper

In a large pot over medium heat, melt butter. Add onion and red pepper and sauté for 4 minutes. Thoroughly whisk in flour, cream, and milk. Heat mixture until thickened, about 3 minutes. Add shrimp, chicken stock, and tomato paste. Heat until shrimp have cooked through, about 5 minutes. Using a hand blender, purée soup until it has a creamy texture. Season with salt and pepper to taste.

Serve hot with crusty bread.

Cream of Mushroom Soup

Makes 12 Servings

½ pound butter
1 small white onion, chopped
2 cups flour
1 cup mushrooms, puréed
1 cup mushrooms, sliced
1 tablespoon salt
1 tablespoon black pepper
1 pint heavy cream
1 (16-ounce) can beef broth
½ gallon of milk

In a large soup pot, melt butter over medium heat. Add onions and cook until they are opaque. Whisk in flour and cook 4 minutes (still over medium heat). Add puréed and sliced mushrooms, salt, pepper, heavy cream, beef broth, and milk. Cook until thick.

Serve hot with bread of choice.

Loaded Potato Soup

Makes 12 Servings

½ pound butter
1 tablespoon onion powder
1 small bag frozen hash brown potatoes
2 cups flour
1 quart heavy whipping cream
½ gallon milk
1 (16-ounce) can chicken broth
1 tablespoon salt
2 tablespoons white pepper

Toppings:
Bacon bits
Scallions, chopped
Shredded Cheddar cheese

In a large soup pot, melt butter over medium heat. Add the onions and sauté until they are opaque. Add hash brown potatoes to the pot and sauté until they are softened. Whisk in flour and continue cooking over medium for about 4 minutes. Add heavy cream, milk, chicken broth, and spices; continue cooking until the soup is thickened.

Serve the soup topped with bacon bits, scallions, and shredded cheese.

THE STOVALL HOUSE COUNTRY INN & RESTAURANT

The Stovall House Inn and Restaurant are located in a restored 1837 Victorian farmhouse situated on a knoll overlooking the Sautee Valley and the surrounding mountains. The inn has five

guest rooms, each with their own private baths featuring old-fashioned pull-chain toilets and pedestal sinks. Décor throughout the home is in keeping with the authentic old-time feel of an intimate country inn.

Owner Hamilton Schwartz painstakingly restored the home in 1983, a fourteen-month effort that involved transforming the top level of the house into lodging accommodations and adding the restaurant on the bottom level. In 2005, the home and its 26 acres of land were placed in a land trust ensuring that a little piece of historical, rural America will be preserved indefinitely.

INNKEEPER:	Hamilton Schwartz
ADDRESS:	1526 Highway 225 North, Sautee-Nacoochee, Ga 30571
TELEPHONE:	(706) 878-3355
E-MAIL:	info@stovallhouse.com
WEBSITE:	www.stovallhouse.com
ROOMS:	5 Rooms; Private baths
CHILDREN:	Children age 1 and older welcome
PETS:	Not allowed

Tomato Herb Soup

Makes 16 Servings

*"This is our old reliable soup that we use for group luncheons.
It goes great with our infamous Cheese Muffins – sorry, that recipe
is a secret so you'll have to come here for them."*

—INNKEEPER, *The Stovall House Country Inn*

1½ cups olive oil
2 cups onion, chopped
3 cups celery, chopped
½ cup flour
2 quarts water
46 ounces V8
1 (10-pound) can whole peeled tomatoes
2 tablespoons parsley
2 tablespoons sugar
1 teaspoon thyme
½ teaspoon pepper
2 bay leaves
1 tablespoon basil

In a large pot, heat the oil over medium-high heat and sauté the
onion and celery. Stir in the flour until well mixed. Add the water
and V8 and stir to mix. Grind the canned tomatoes and add them
to the soup along with the remaining ingredients. Simmer until
the soup is heated through and flavors have combined.

Garnish with Parmesan cheese and parsley flakes to serve.

THE PARTRIDGE INN

Set on a hilltop in historic Summerville, just minutes from downtown Augusta sits the historic Partridge Inn. With 145 guest rooms, studios and suites, each finely appointed with luxurious

amenities, an award-winning restaurant, bar with live jazz, private courtyard pool, and excellent service, it's easy to see just how this renowned hotel has managed to remain one of Georgia's most popular vacation retreats.

The elegant and stately Partridge Inn was the first hotel in Georgia selected for inclusion in Historic Hotels of America. For over 100 years, this luxury hotel has reigned as one of the country's premier resort destinations. As such, the Partridge Inn has played host to a virtual who's who of the country's celebrities. Amongst the many, some of the most well known include Ty Cobb, Bob Dylan, James Brown, and President Warren G. Harding.

INNKEEPER: Jeff Brower

ADDRESS: 2110 Walton Way, Augusta, Georgia 30904

TELEPHONE: (706) 737-8888; (800) 476-6888

E-MAIL: info@partridgeinn.com

WEBSITE: www.partridgeinn.com

ROOMS: 120 Rooms; 24 Suites; 1 Penthouse; Private baths

CHILDREN: Welcome

PETS: Welcome

Baby Spinach Salad with Strawberry-Ginger Dressing

Makes 4 Servings

16 ounces baby spinach, washed
8 ounces crumbled goat cheese
4 strawberries, sliced
¼ cup candied pecans

Strawberry-Ginger Dressing:
1 cup strawberries, sliced
¼ cup rice wine vinegar
1 tablespoon ginger, minced
1 tablespoon sugar
1 cup grapeseed oil

For the dressing: Combine all ingredients except the oil in a blender. Incorporate on low speed. Slowly add your oil, while continuing to blend. Adjust seasonings with salt and pepper.

For the salad: Toss the spinach in a bowl with goat cheese, strawberries, and pecans. Add 1 ounce of dressing and season with salt and pepper. Place the salad in the center of a serving bowl and arrange to show the strawberries and cheese.

Skelton House

Located in beautiful Hartwell, Georgia, the Skelton House is an elegant bed and breakfast that combines modern comfort and grace with history and tradition. Each of the seven guest rooms re-flects a different theme ranging from the Victorian inspired Annie's Grace Room and the youthful Bunk Room to the warm and cozy Mama and Papa's Room.

The inn's expansive gardens are not to be missed. You can take a relaxing stroll and enjoy the peaceful surroundings, or you can settle in with a cup of coffee and watch the sunset.

INNKEEPERS:	Ruth & John Skelton
ADDRESS:	97 Benson Street, Hartwell, Georgia 30643
TELEPHONE:	(706) 376-7969
E-MAIL:	info@theskeltonhouse.com
WEBSITE:	www.theskeltonhouse.com
ROOMS:	7 Rooms
CHILDREN:	Welcome
PETS:	Not allowed

Skelton House Chicken Salad

Makes 6 Servings

Dressing:
¾ cups vegetable oil
$\frac{1}{3}$ cup white vinegar
2 Ramen Noodle seasoning packets

Salad:
1 cup raisins, cranberries, or craisins
½ cup sesame seeds
½ cup sliced almonds
1 rotisserie chicken, skinned and boned,
    meat chopped
$\frac{1}{3}$ cup chopped green onion
2 (12-ounce) bags broccoli slaw
1 red delicious apple, chopped

For the dressing: In a small bowl, whisk together the oil, vinegar, and ramen noodle seasoning packets.

For the salad: In a large bowl, toss together all salad ingredients and prepared dressing. Top the salad with crumbled raw ramen noodles and serve.

THE FORSYTH PARK INN

The historic Forsyth Park Inn, located in Savannah's historic district, will envelop quests in its classic Southern charm. This Queen Anne Victorian mansion overlooks Savannah's beautiful Forsyth Park and is a member of the Historic Inns of Savannah. The inn has been featured on the Travel Channel and is said to be home to the ghost of Lottie Churchill, a woman whose spirit remains unsettled after 117 years.

Each elegantly appointed guest room features antique Victorian décor and amenities ranging from four-poster beds, wet bars, whirlpool tubs, working fireplaces, and courtyard or park views. Luxury soaps, lotions, and cozy robes are provided for each guest to encourage a relaxing and rejuvenating vacation experience.

INNKEEPERS: Rick & Lori Blass

ADDRESS: 102 West Hall Street, Savannah, Georgia 31401

TELEPHONE: (912) 233-6804

E-MAIL: innkeeper@forsythparkinn.com

WEBSITE: www.forsythparkinn.com

ROOMS: 11 Rooms; 1 Cottage; Private baths

CHILDREN: Children age 12 and older welcome

PETS: Welcome; Call ahead; Resident pets

Shrimp Salad in a Croustade

Makes 8 Servings

*"This is one of our guests' favorites,
with Ms. Ozella's special touch, of course."*

—INNKEEPER, *Forsyth Inn*

Croustade:
1 (1 pound) loaf thinly sliced bread
3 tablespoons unsalted butter

Shrimp Salad:
1 pound fresh shrimp, cleaned and
    heads and tails removed
3 green onions, chopped
2 tablespoons fresh chopped parsley
½ cup finely chopped celery
½ lemon juiced
1 teaspoon garlic pepper
1¼ teaspoon Lawry's seasoning
1¼ cup Blue Plate mayonnaise
2 hard boiled eggs, diced

For the croustade: Preheat oven to 375°F. Remove the crusts
from the bread and cut each slice in half. Butter both sides of the
bread and press each half into the cups of a mini muffin tin. Bake
15–20 minutes, until the edges are golden.

For the shrimp salad: Boil the shrimp for 2–4 minutes (depending
on size). Drain and chop coarsely. In a medium bowl, combine
the shrimp with the other salad ingredients. Cover with plastic
wrap and refrigerate for 2 hours before spooning into the pre-made
croustades.

Luncheon & Dinner Entrées

Luncheon & Dinner Entrées

> "One cannot think well,
> love well, sleep well,
> if one has not dined well.
>
> —VIRGINIA WOOLF

THE BEECHWOOD INN

The Beechwood Inn offers luxury accommodations in a serene and rustic mountain setting. 100-year-old terraced gardens and Black Rock Mountain surround the inn making it feel as though you really have stepped into another world. Guests at the inn are treated to a mouthwatering gourmet breakfast, "wine-thirty" the inn's wine hour, complimentary soft drinks, and homemade cookies. Each of the airy guest rooms has its own working fireplace, antique décor and rugs, folk art, and period furniture.

*"Many people avoid the typical "bed and breakfast," fearing that the service or quality will be lacking compared to the typical luxury hotel chain.... Others worry that privacy will be sacrificed. No worries here. You will receive superb service and food on par with either the Ritz or Four Seasons, and at a much more reasonable rate. The inn is beautiful and the accommodations are first-rate and peaceful. You will have all the privacy you want, and without the canned "my pleasure" you received from the luxury chains." —*GUEST

INNKEEPERS: David & Gayle Darugh

ADDRESS: 220 Beechwood Drive, Clayton, Georgia 30525

TELEPHONE: (706) 782-5485; (866) 782-2485

E-MAIL: david-gayle@beechwoodinn.ws

WEBSITE: www.beechwoodinn.ws

ROOMS: 2 Rooms; 5 Suites; 1 Cottage; Private baths

CHILDREN: Children age 12 and older welcome

PETS: Dogs welcome; Resident pets

Brined Niman Ranch Frenched Pork Chops

Makes 12 Servings

"Plan ahead, the pork will need to brine overnight."

—INNKEEPER, *Beechwood Inn*

Brine:

2 cups kosher salt	2 tablespoons fresh thyme,
¾ cup sugar	chopped
3 tablespoons Cajun seasoning	12 garlic cloves, smashed
2 teaspoons red pepper flakes	2–3 bay leaves
2 tablespoons juniper berries	3 quarts water
¼ cup fresh rosemary, chopped	

12 Niman Ranch Frenched center cut pork chops,
about 1½-inch thick*
Fresh ground black pepper
3 tablespoons chopped rosemary, thyme, and sage
3 tablespoons olive oil, for grilling

Mix all of the brine ingredients together in a large non-reactive pot and bring to a boil. Remove from heat and stir to ensure the salt and sugar have dissolved. Let the brine cool and put in the refrigerator to chill. Once it is cold, submerge the pork chops, cover and refrigerate overnight.

The following morning: Remove the pork from the brine and pat dry – do not rinse. Preheat your gas grill on high. Season the chops with pepper and fresh herbs and brush with olive oil. Sear the chops directly over the grill for about 1½ minutes per side. Lower heat to medium-low and cook chops to desired doneness. We recommend you serve these medium rare, or when the chops reach an internal temperature of 140–145°F.

*Niman Ranch offers online ordering for their hormone free meats at www.nimanranch.com

Southern Cross Guest Ranch

This all-inclusive bed and breakfast is also a family-owned and operated horse farm. Of course, horseback riding is the featured activity at the ranch, and they even offer riding lessons for beginners. Group tours and individual rides are both offered. After a day's ride, guests can relax in the pool, soak in the hot tub, or even indulge themselves in an aqua massage.

"This is the most wonderful place! Every single aspect is inviting and comfortable! I've never been anywhere I felt so relaxed and welcome. The riding was great, the food outstanding, and the staff was awesome. Thank you so much for the best vacation I've ever had!" —GUEST

INNKEEPER: Noel Detienne
ADDRESS: 1670 Bethany Church Road, Madison, Georgia 30650
TELEPHONE: (706) 342-8027
E-MAIL: mail@southcross.com
WEBSITE: www.southcross.com
ROOMS: 16 Rooms; Private baths
CHILDREN: Children age 4 and older welcome
PETS: Not allowed; Resident pets

Cowboy Spaghetti

Makes 4 Servings

1 pound spaghetti
Salt
1 tablespoon extra-virgin olive oil
3 slices smoky bacon, chopped
1 pound ground sirloin
1 medium onion, chopped
3–4 garlic cloves, chopped
Salt and ground black pepper, to taste
2 teaspoons hot sauce
1 tablespoon Worcestershire sauce
½ cup beer
1 (14-ounce) can chopped or
    crushed fire-roasted tomatoes
1 (8-ounce) can tomato sauce
8 ounces sharp Cheddar
4 scallions

Bring a large pot of water to a boil; add spaghetti and salt and cook until pasta is al dente. Remove spaghetti from heat and drain.

While the spaghetti cooks, heat a deep skillet over medium-high heat. Add extra-virgin olive oil and bacon to the skillet; brown and crisp bacon, about 5 minutes. Remove bacon with a slotted spoon and drain off excess fat if necessary, leave just enough grease to coat the bottom of the skillet. Add beef to the skillet and crumble as it browns, about 3-4 minutes. Stir onion and garlic into the meat and season with salt, pepper, hot sauce, and Worcestershire sauce. Add the beer and deglaze the pan. Cook meat mixture about 5 minutes longer and then add tomatoes and tomato sauce. Add the hot spaghetti to the sauce and stir to combine. Adjust seasonings and serve.

Top with grated cheese, chopped scallions, and crumbled bacon.

Tasty Cabbage Rolls

Makes 8 Servings

1 large (or 2 small) cabbages
1 pound ground beef
2 cups cooked rice
5 green onions, chipped (or 1 mild onion)
4 cloves garlic, minced
Pepper, to taste
1/3 cup low-sodium chicken broth
1 (15-ounce) can tomato sauce
1 (6-ounce) can Italian style or regular tomato paste
1 (28-ounce) can whole tomatoes,
    broken in half with a spoon (do not drain)
$\frac{1}{3}$ cup brown sugar
Juice of 1 lemon

Preheat oven to 325°F. Core cabbage and add to a large pot filled half-way with water. Bring to a boil and cover pot; boil about 20 minutes, until leaves are softened. Drain on paper towels. While the cabbage is boiling, blend beef, cooked rice, green onions, garlic, pepper, and ¼ cup of chicken broth. Place the remaining chicken broth, tomato sauce, tomato paste, whole tomatoes with juice, brown sugar, and lemon juice in a medium-sized roasting pan. Stir well to blend.

Separate 30-32 leaves from the cabbage and lay them out on a cutting board. Take a rounded tablespoon of the meat mixture and place it in the center of the leaf. Tuck the sides of the leaf in and roll, starting with the thicker part and ending with the thinner. Place seam-side-down in a roasting pan. Repeat with remaining leaves and beef mixture. Spoon tomato sauce over the cabbage rolls and cover the roasting pan. Bake 1–1½ hours, or until beef is completely cooked.

Southern Almond Chicken

Makes 6 Servings

6 boneless, skinless chicken breasts
½ teaspoon salt
$\frac{1}{8}$ teaspoon pepper
3 tablespoons butter, divided
1½ cups whipping cream
2 tablespoons orange marmalade
1 tablespoon Dijon mustard
$\frac{1}{8}$ teaspoon ground red pepper
1 (2¼-ounce) package sliced almonds, toasted

Place chicken breasts between two sheets of heavy-duty plastic wrap and flatten to ¼-inch thickness using a mallet or rolling pin. Sprinkle the chicken with salt and pepper.

Melt 1½ tablespoons butter in a large skillet over medium-high heat. Add half of the chicken and cook 2 minutes on each side, or until golden brown. Remove from skillet and repeat with remaining chicken. Reduce heat to medium. Add whipping cream, marmalade, mustard, and red pepper to the skillet, stirring well. Return the chicken to the skillet and sprinkle with almonds. Cook 8 minutes, or until sauce thickens.

Serve over rice or mashed potatoes.

WISTERIA HALL

The stately Wisteria Hall is truly a sight to behold. This historic home is one of the most magnificent buildings of its era that has now been fully renovated to allow for guests as well as special formal occasions. The inn's location is also great for vacationers seeking a little bit of Southern hospitality and history.

Waynesboro, Georgia, is the seat of Burke County – one of the original eight counties in Georgia. It is said that George Washing-

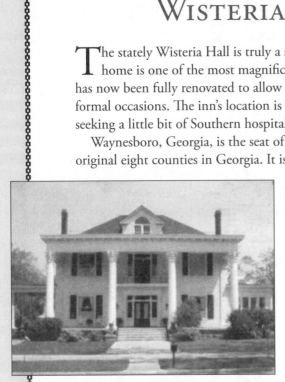

ton himself owned land in Waynesboro before building his home in Mount Vernon. Today, visitors can relive the history of this town by visiting the many historic sites. Learn more about the town at the Waynesboro-Burke County Museum, visit the Di-Lane Plantation and Wimberly House, take a walking tour of historic downtown, and visit the Confederate Memorial Cemetery and the Burke County Library to brush up on your Civil War knowledge. Waynesboro also has great antique shopping. Outdoor activities in the area include golfing, and boating. Burke County is also one of the biggest hot spots for hunting and fishing.

INNKEEPERS:	Ralph & Nancy Lynn
ADDRESS:	824 Myrick Street, Waynesboro, Georgia 30830
TELEPHONE:	(706) 437-1323
E-MAIL:	wisteriahall@comcast.net
WEBSITE:	www.wisteriahallonline.com
ROOMS:	4 Rooms; Private baths
CHILDREN:	Children age 10 and older welcome
PETS:	Not allowed

Chicken Breasts with Cream Sauce

Makes 6 Servings

"This dish is very popular with lunch and dinner guests at the B&B." —INNKEEPER, *Wisteria Hall, Waynesboro*

6 boneless, skinless chicken breasts
Onion and chive cream cheese
1 (10 ¾-ounce) can cream of chicken soup
½ cup mayonnaise
1 sleeve Ritz crackers, crushed
Shredded Cheddar cheese (optional)

Preheat oven to 350°F. Wash and pat dry the chicken. Cut the chicken to make a small pouch and place 1 tablespoon of the cream cheese into each chicken breast. Place the chicken breasts in a 13x9-inch baking dish.

In a medium bowl, combine the soup and mayonnaise; spread mixture over the chicken breasts and sprinkle with the crushed crackers and cheddar cheese. Bake 30-45 minutes until chicken is cooked through.

THE STOVALL
HOUSE COUNTRY INN &
RESTAURANT

Afﬁter loving and painstaking restorations, Stovall House Country
Inn and Restaurant made its debut as a true country inn in
1983. The inn's restaurant opened its doors to the public on Labor
Day the following year. The restaurant is open to guests as well as
the general public and features regional cuisine made from fresh and
local ingredients.

Dinner is served Thursday through Saturday, but the restaurant is
also available for large luncheon and dinner parties with just 48 hours
notice. Entrées include fresh crab-stuffed trout, Tilapia Almondine,
lamb chops, and pasta primavera, and you'll definitely want to save
room for dessert, or a Sweet Afterthought. Mouthwatering selections
range from apple praline pie to the chocolate fudge brownie served
with ice cream and fudge sauce.

INNKEEPER:	Hamilton Schwartz
ADDRESS:	1526 Highway 225 North, Sautee-Nacoochee, Georgia 30571
TELEPHONE:	(706) 878-3355
E-MAIL:	info@stovallhouse.com
WEBSITE:	www.stovallhouse.com
ROOMS:	5 Rooms; Private baths
CHILDREN:	Children age 1 and older welcome
PETS:	Not allowed

Stuffed Chicken Breast

Makes 8 Servings

"This entrée has been on our menu since we opened the restaurant in 1984. It is our 'house specialty' and our most requested entrée."

—INNKEEPER, *Stovall House Country Inn*

8 (6-8 ounce) boneless skinless chicken breasts
All-purpose flour
Egg wash
Herbed bread crumbs
3 tablespoons canola oil

Cream Cheese Herb Stuffing:
1 pound cream cheese
1 tablespoon basil
1 tablespoon chives
1 tablespoon dill
1 tablespoon chopped garlic

For the cream cheese herb stuffing: Soften the cream cheese, add herbs and mix well to combine.

For the chicken: Preheat oven to 350°F. Trim the chicken and cut a pocket into each breast. Stuff with 1 heaping tablespoon of the herb stuffing mixture. Set out three shallow dishes, one with flour, one with egg wash, and one with bread crumbs. Dredge each breast in the flour, then dip in the egg wash and roll in the bread crumbs. Heat the Canola oil in a large skillet and sauté each breast until browned. Place the sautéed chicken on a greased baking pan and bake in the oven for about 20 minutes.

THE WINDOWS INN B&B

Innkeepers Lyle and Janis Lewis want to make each and every guest at the Windows Inn Bed & Breakfast feel welcome and relaxed – like you're part of the family. They enjoy providing their guests with "good ole Southern hospitality" and promise that your stay at Windows Inn will be a memorable one.

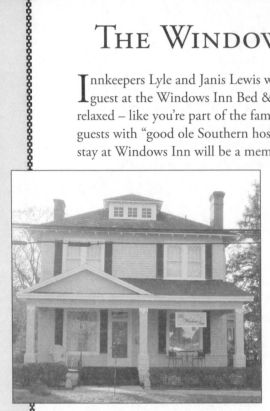

The quiet town of McRae offers travelers the opportunity to step back and relax. There are a variety of local activities available including fishing, antiquing, biking, and golf. There are also a number of historical sites in the area including the Little Ocmulgee State Park. Park activities include canoe and pedal boat rentals, skiing, and swimming.

INNKEEPERS:	Lyle & Janis Lewis
ADDRESS:	206 South 4th Avenue, McRae, Georgia 31055
TELEPHONE:	(229) 868-2067
E-MAIL:	jklewis1@windstream.net
WEBSITE:	www.thewindowsinn.com
ROOMS:	4 Rooms; Private & shared baths
CHILDREN:	Children age 12 and older welcome
PETS:	Not allowed

Chicken Caesar Lasagna

Makes 9–12 Servings

"This dish is one my family and guests request
most often for evening meals. The recipe was adapted
from one found in Better Homes and Gardens. *"*

—INNKEEPER, *The Windows Inn Bed & Breakfast*

9 whole wheat or regular lasagna noodles
2 (10-ounce) containers Alfredo sauce
3 tablespoons lemon juice
¼ teaspoon black pepper
3 cups cooked chicken
1 (10-ounce) package frozen chopped spinach,
    thawed and well-drained
1 cup bottled roasted red sweet peppers,
    drained and chopped
¼ cup shredded Italian cheese blend

Preheat oven to 325°F. Cook the noodles according to package directions, drain, rinse with cold water, and drain again. Meanwhile, in a small bowl, combine Alfredo sauce, lemon juice, and black pepper. Stir in the chicken, spinach, and red peppers.

Lightly coat a 3-quart rectangular baking dish with non-stick cooking spray. Arrange 3 noodles in the bottom of the dish and top with ⅓ of the chicken mixture. Repeat layers twice. Cover and bake 45–55 minutes, or until heated through. Uncover and sprinkle with cheese. Bake uncovered for an additional 5 minutes, until cheese is melted. Let stand 15 minutes before serving.

Shellmont Inn

Built in 1891, the stately Shellmont Inn is the picture of Southern grace and hospitality. Stained glass, intricately carved woodwork, period antiques, oriental rugs, and elegant wall treatments can be found throughout the home. The guest rooms are airy and spacious and the common areas are warm and inviting. The inn is conveniently located just minutes away from Atlanta's theaters,

fine dining, and historic district. Tennis, biking, historic walking tours, the Atlanta Botanical Gardens, and Zoo-Atlanta are just a few of the attractions located around the area,

Begin your day with a hearty breakfast featuring seasonal specialties prepared by the inn's resident chef. After that, take your pick of local activities. When you return, relax on the front porch and enjoy a Southern sunset before retiring to your room.

INNKEEPERS:	Debbie & Ed McCord
ADDRESS:	821 Piedmont Avenue, NE, Atlanta, Georgia 30308
TELEPHONE:	(404) 872-9290
E-MAIL:	innkeeper@shellmont.com
WEBSITE:	www.shellmont.com
ROOMS:	6 Rooms; 2 Suites; 1 Cottage; Private baths
CHILDREN:	Welcome; Call ahead
PETS:	Not allowed; Resident pets

Sue's Chicken &
Mashed Potatoes

Makes 6 Servings

*"We were fortunate to open Shellmont next to a
wonderful neighbor (Sue) who advanced my cooking skills.
All of our guests should be thankful! This was a favorite of Sue's."*
— INNKEEPER, *Shellmont Inn*

6 chicken breasts, skin left on
6 tablespoons Italian dressing
6 slices of bacon, each cut in half

Mashed Potatoes:
6–8 large boiling potatoes
½ cup butter
Salt and pepper, to taste

For the chicken: Preheat oven to 350°F. Wash and dry the chicken breasts and place skin-side-down in a 9x13-inch baking dish. Season with salt and pepper and drizzle 1 tablespoon of Italian dressing over each breast. Place a large portion of the mashed potatoes over each breast. Place two strips of bacon (1 halved slice) over the top of the potatoes. Bake for 1 hour, occasionally basting with pan juices. Potatoes should be golden brown.

For the potatoes: Boil and drain the potatoes. Mash with butter. Do not add cream or milk to these potatoes.

Turkey Mountain Chili

Makes 6 Servings

"We developed this recipe as a healthier alternative to traditional beef chili."

—INNKEEPER, *Shellmont Inn*

1 pound ground turkey breast
1 medium onion, chopped
1 clove garlic, minced
1 green pepper, chopped
2 (15-ounce) cans chopped tomatoes
2 (15-ounce) cans whole tomatoes
2 (15-ounce) cans dark kidney beans
2 (15-ounce) cans black beans
1 tablespoon Worcestershire sauce
1 tablespoon vinegar
1 teaspoon dry mustard
$\frac{1}{3}$ teaspoon black pepper
$\frac{2}{3}$ teaspoons red pepper
½ teaspoon chili powder

In a large pot, brown turkey meat with onion, garlic, and green pepper – you may need to add a little olive oil to the pot to keep ingredients from sticking to the bottom. Once the meat is fully cooked, drain any excess juices. Add all of the remaining ingredients to the pot and allow to simmer over low heat for several hours.

As an alternative, once you have cooked your turkey as above, pour all of the ingredients into a crock-pot set on low heat to cook for several hours.

Flounder with Walnut Topping

Makes 4 Servings

½ cup chopped walnuts
2 tablespoons plain bread crumbs
1 tablespoon apricot jam
1 tablespoon balsamic vinegar
4 (4-ounce) pieces of flounder

Preheat oven to 400°F. In a small bowl, combine walnuts and bread crumbs and set aside. In a separate bowl, combine apricot jam and vinegar. Wash and dry each piece of flounder before brushing each side with the jam mixture. Dredge the flounder in the bread mixture and place in a baking dish sprayed with non-stick cooking spray. Bake 12–18 minutes.

Did you know that fresh flounder is renowned for its delicate flavor and tender but firm texture? It's also very low in fat. Special care must be taken to ensure that you do not overcook this fish or it will dry out. Flounder does, however, lend itself well to a multitude of cooking methods.

GLEN-ELLA SPRINGS
COUNTRY INN

This historic mountain inn has been continuously recognized as one of Georgia's top 10 dining destinations as well as one of the state's best bed and breakfasts. The inn's dinner menu features a wide variety of items including Blue Cheese Stuffed Beef Tenderloin, Herb Crusted Rack of New Zealand Lamb, and Cedar Planked Salmon. And, since the restaurant features some of the best food in the area, you'll definitely want to try one of the homemade

desserts. Classic Crème Brûlée, Key Lime Pie, and Apple Bread Pudding are just a few of the delectable items waiting for you.

The rustic and peaceful setting is perfect for a romantic weekend with a loved one, a large family get together, or just a quiet weekend enjoying the mountain air. Each of the inn's guest rooms features heart-pine paneled walls and ceilings. Décor consists of period antiques, handmade crafts, and cozy chintzes. Each room opens up onto one of the inn's common porches where you can sit and enjoy the serene setting while rocking in one of the chairs and sipping iced tea.

INNKEEPERS:	Barrie & Bobby Aycock
ADDRESS:	1789 Bear Gap Road, Clarkesville, Georgia 30523
TELEPHONE:	(706) 754-7295; (888) 455-8786
E-MAIL:	meetings@glenella.com
WEBSITE:	www.glenella.com
ROOMS:	12 Rooms; 4 Suites; Private baths
CHILDREN:	Welcome
PETS:	Not allowed

Grilled Tuna with Orange Ginger Sauce

Makes 4 Servings

1 cup fresh orange juice
1 teaspoon Dijon mustard
6 tablespoons extra-virgin olive oil
2½ teaspoons fresh ginger, minced
Salt and pepper, to taste
4 (6-ounce) top quality, fresh tuna steaks

In a small, heavy saucepan, bring the orange juice to a boil and reduce over medium heat – until about ⅓ cup remains. Turn the heat to low and whisk in mustard and oil. Stir in ginger and season with salt and pepper. Remove from heat and set aside.*

Grill the tuna steaks to desired doneness and drizzle with the sauce to serve.

*Sauce will keep in the fridge for 1-2 days. Allow it to come to room temperature before using. This sauce is also good as a dressing over spinach salad.

THE PARTRIDGE INN

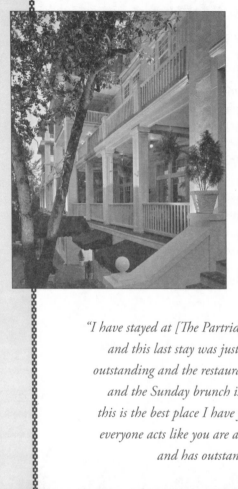

For over a century, the Partridge Inn has served as a tranquil retreat for society's most elite. Originally built in 1836 and established as a hotel in 1892, this historic inn has recently undergone extensive renovations returning the venerable property to the luster and prominence of its heyday. The Partridge Inn is renowned for its charming Southern details - more than a quarter-mile of beautiful verandahs, classic columns, stately magnolia trees and unparalleled personal service – as well as its fine culinary program and genuine southern hospitality.

"I have stayed at [The Partridge Inn] many times over the last 20 years and this last stay was just as good as all the others. The hotel is outstanding and the restaurants are amazing. Their food is excellent and the Sunday brunch is a must. If you are going to Augusta, this is the best place I have found to stay. The staff is very pleasant; everyone acts like you are a VIP…All in all, this hotel is amazing and has outstanding amenities." —GUEST

INNKEEPER: Jeff Brower
ADDRESS: 2110 Walton Way, Augusta, Georgia 30904
TELEPHONE: (706) 737-8888; (800) 476-6888
E-MAIL: info@partridgeinn.com
WEBSITE: www.partridgeinn.com
ROOMS: 120 Rooms; 24 Suites; 1 Penthouse; Private baths
CHILDREN: Welcome
PETS: Welcome

Bourbon BBQ Glazed Salmon

Makes 4 Servings

4 7-ounce salmon filets

Bourbon BBQ Glaze:
2 tablespoons olive oil
1 yellow onion, diced small
2 cloves minced garlic
1 teaspoon paprika
1 teaspoon cumin
1 teaspoon curry powder
1 teaspoon Coleman's dry mustard
¼ cup apple cider vinegar
¼ cup molasses
½ cup bourbon
4 cups ketchup

For the glaze: In a large saucepan or skillet, sweat the onion and garlic in 2 tablespoons olive oil. Add the dry spices and sauté 2 minutes. Add remaining ingredients and simmer 35 minutes. Blend and cool completely.

For the salmon: Season each filet with salt and pepper and grill to cook. Coat cooked salmon with BBQ sauce and place under a broiler for just under a minute. Serve with mashed potatoes and vegetables.

Roussell's Garden B&B

This lovely Queen Anne Victorian, originally built in 1888, opened its doors as a luxury bed & breakfast in 2005 after loving restorations. Elegance and charm abound in this beautiful home, surrounded by lush gardens filled with blooming vines and flowers, citrus and fig trees. Inside, guests will delight in the mixture of period furnishings and modern conveniences. Hardwood floors, graceful 12-foot ceilings, stained glass, and chandeliers - all traditional aspects of Victorian-era homes - can be found throughout, lending an air of historic grace to Roussell's Garden.

"I am a frequent guest at b&bs, in fact, I own a b&b and Roussell's Garden is just great! For me there are certain things I want when I stay at a b&b and this place has it all – wireless internet, luxury linens, cable TV, beautiful common space, and a full breakfast. I am not an easy guest and I would recommend this b&b to anyone!" —Guest

INNKEEPERS: Bryan & Janet Roussell

ADDRESS: 208 East Henry Street, Savannah, Georgia 31401

TELEPHONE: (912) 239-1415

E-MAIL: info@roussellsgarden.com

WEBSITE: www.roussellsgarden.com

ROOMS: 3 Rooms; Private & shared baths

CHILDREN: Cannot accommodate

PETS: Not allowed

Baked Pecan Fish

Makes 8–12 Servings

1 onion, sliced
2–3 pounds of fish filets
½ cup crushed pecans
¼ cup bread crumbs
¼ cup Parmesan cheese
Salt and pepper, to taste
Garlic powder, optional
3–4 tablespoons melted butter
    or olive oil

Preheat oven to 350°F. Spray a 9x13-inch baking pan with non-stick cooking spray. Lay the onion slices over the bottom of the pan. Place the fish filets on top of the onions. In a small bowl, mix together bread crumbs, Parmesan cheese, pecans, salt, pepper, and garlic powder. Sprinkle mixture over fish and drizzle with melted butter or olive oil. Cover and bake approximately 20-23 minutes, until fish flakes. Cook time will be determined by amount of fish.

COLUMBIA SQUARE INN

The quiet and private setting of the Columbia Square Inn make it a truly unique lodging experience located right in the heart of Savannah. After extensive renovations, the Columbia Square Inn was awarded the Historic Savannah Foundation's Preservation Award for its outstanding work in preserving the city's historic and cultural heritage.

"We had the most romantic three days in Savannah, mostly due to the hospitality of the owners of the Columbia Square Inn. They made us feel like we were family. The rooms were beautiful, and breakfast in our room was delicious. They even kept us supplied in Diet Coke! I would love to visit again…"

—GUEST

INNKEEPER: Barbara Wall Fricks

ADDRESS: 125 Habersham Street, Savannah, Georgia 31401

TELEPHONE: (912) 236-0444

E-MAIL: N/A

WEBSITE: www.columbiasquareinn.com

ROOMS: 3 Rooms; 1 Suite; Private baths

CHILDREN: Cannot accommodate

PETS: Not allowed

Savannah Seafood Quiche

Makes 6-8 Servings

1 unbaked pie shell
1 can drained crab
1 cup cooked shrimp
½ cup scallops
6 beaten eggs
1 cup whipping cream
2 teaspoons diced onion
2 teaspoons diced green bell pepper
2 teaspoon diced red bell pepper
½ teaspoon salt
¼ teaspoon pepper
8 ounces shredded mild Cheddar cheese

Preheat oven to 375°F. In a medium bowl, combine crab, shrimp, and scallops; set aside. In a separate medium bowl, beat the eggs and add whipping cream, onion, bell peppers, salt, and pepper. Blend well and pour into the pie shell. Spread cheese evenly over the top of the egg mixture. Gently pour the seafood mixture over the cheese. Bake 40-50 minutes until a knife inserted in the center comes away clean.

THE FITZPATRICK HOTEL

The Fitzpatrick Hotel is a grand old historic place that has been in operation since it was built in 1900. The inn combines classic period décor and luxury accommodations with modern conveniences and amenities. Rooms feature working gas fireplaces, antique claw tubs, and antique furniture including wrought iron and oak beds. A continental breakfast is included with your stay and the inn's courtyard, conference room, and Grand Ballroom are all available for private functions.

Downstairs, the inn has its very own bar and lounge – the perfect place for a before or after dinner drink with family and friends. Every Sunday at the Fitzpatrick, guests will enjoy a Southern country-style brunch buffet with omelet and carving stations. The inn also features its own restaurant, the Down Under. Menu items at the Down Under include fresh seafood, gourmet burgers, and Certified Angus beef.

INNKEEPER: Tom Jones
ADDRESS: 16 West Square, Washington, Georgia 30673
TELEPHONE: (706) 678-5900
E-MAIL: info@thefitzpatrickhotel.com
WEBSITE: http://thefitzpatrickhotel.com
ROOMS: 16 Rooms; 1 Suite; Private baths
CHILDREN: Welcome
PETS: Not allowed

Down Under Pasta

Makes 1 Serving

4 ounces cooked fettuccine
1 tablespoon unsalted butter
1 teaspoon olive oil
1 teaspoon diced onion
½ teaspoon freshly chopped garlic
1 (21/25 size) shrimp
1 teaspoon Old Bay seasoning
2 ounces white wine
2 ounces heavy cream
1 pinch dried basil
¼ cup grated Parmesan
Parsley and green onion, chopped for garnish

Boil the fettuccine according to package directions and immediately cool in an ice bath to stop cooking. When the pasta is cold, add 1 teaspoon of oil and a pinch of salt; toss and set aside. In a large sauté pan, heat butter and oil until it shimmers across the pan. Add the onion and cook until softened but not browned. Add the garlic and cook until an aroma is present. Add the shrimp and Old Bay seasoning to the pan and toss to distribute. When the shrimp begin to turn red, add the wine and simmer until the shrimp are almost done, then add the cream and basil. When the cream comes to a low boil, add the Parmesan and cook until mixture begins to bubble. Toss in pasta and serve, garnished with parsley and green onion.

Chicken Florentine with Mushrooms

Makes 2 Servings

2 boneless skinless chicken breasts
5 medium button mushrooms, sliced
2 cups packed fresh spinach leaves
1 tablespoon chopped onion
1 teaspoon chopped garlic
½ ounce pernod or anisette
1 tablespoon olive oil
Salt and pepper to taste
Hollandaise sauce (see next page)

Preheat oven to 350°F. In a heavy skillet over medium-high heat, melt together butter and olive oil until shimmering in pan. Add the chicken and cook until golden brown. Transfer chicken to an oven safe pan and bake until cooked through (about 20 minutes). Using the same skillet, sauté the mushrooms, onion, and garlic and season with salt and pepper. When the vegetables are softened, add the spinach, liqueur, and wine to the pan and allow the liquid to steam the spinach. Once the liquid has almost completely evaporated, add the heavy cream and the Parmesan. Bring mixture to a low boil and simmer briefly.

To serve: Place each chicken breast on a serving plate and divide spinach/mushroom mixture evenly between the two plates. Serve with prepared hollandaise sauce (see next page).

Hollandaise Sauce

Makes approximately 1½ cups

3 egg yolks, as fresh as possible
2 sticks unsalted butter, melted
½ ounce white wine
1 teaspoon lemon juice
Salt, pepper, and cayenne, to taste

Place the fresh egg yolks in a blender and mix until slightly airy and thickened. With the motor running, slowly add the melted butter in a very thin stream until the mixture begins to thicken. Add the wine and lemon juice and continue to add the butter, including milk solids. Season with salt, black pepper, and cayenne pepper, to taste.

Riesling wine is often paired with salmon and hollandaise because of its complementing flavor and refreshing acidity.

Fruit Specialties, Desserts, Cookies, & Bars

Fruit Specialties, Desserts, Cookies, & Bars

*Laughter is brightest
where the food is plentiful
and the company cordial.*

—IRISH PROVERB

MOSSY CREEK AT ASHLEY LANE BED & BRUNCH

Just north of Atlanta, in the North Georgia Mountains, sits Mossy Creek at Ashley Lane Bed & Brunch. The sound of the nearby creeks and the gorgeous views make this a perfect retreat for both nature lovers and the travel weary guest looking to get away from it all. Hiking the Appalachian trail, canoeing, kayaking, tubing, fishing, and gold mine tours are just a few of the area attractions available nearby, or you can relax and enjoy the peace and quiet of the tranquil surroundings.

"You access Mossy Creek by a small mountain road swerving through the meanders of its gentle and enchanting waters. The trees hover over you and start their embrace as soon as you release the effervescence of daily live…Mossy Creek is welcoming you home." —GUEST

INNKEEPER: Eugene D. Frazier

ADDRESS: 971 Mountain Cove Road, Dahlonega, Georgia 30533

TELEPHONE: (706) 865-1550; (404) 791-6653

E-MAIL: ef@mossycreekb-b.com

WEBSITE: www.mossycreekb-b.com

ROOMS: 6 Rooms; 1 Suite; Private & shared baths

CHILDREN: Cannot accommodate

PETS: Not allowed

Mossy Creek Berry Fruit Topping

Makes 4–6 servings

"The vibrant color already indicates the passion you will experience with this topping. You smell the aroma of the warm berries as you pour them on your freshly made waffles. By now you have started salivating. Then silence ... such richness, such savor. A morning brunch you will always remember."

—GUEST, *Mossy Creek at Ashley Lane Bed & Brunch*

3 cups fresh fruit*, any combination of
    blueberries, blackberries, raspberries,
    and strawberries
9 tablespoons water
¼ cup brown sugar
⅓ cup honey
⅓ cup corn syrup

Place berries and water in a medium saucepan; add in the brown sugar, honey, and corn syrup. Bring mixture to a boil, stirring constantly. Reduce heat and simmer, covered, for approximately 10 minutes. Remove lid and let stand for 5-7 minutes.

Serve topping hot over waffles, pancakes, hot biscuits, or French toast with a sprinkle of powdered sugar.

*When fresh berries are not in season, frozen whole berries will work just as well.

Virginia Highland B&B

Virginia Highland B&B is a historic Atlanta home that has been completely renovated to include elegant guest accommodations. In addition to the eclectic décor, welcoming atmosphere, friendly hostess, and comfortable guest rooms, this inn features one of the most unique and amazing gardens in all of Atlanta. Adele and her green thumb have recently earned top recognition as her garden has just been designated an official Audubon Wildlife Sanctuary. When in season, you'll bask in the colorful sights, smells, and sounds of the animals that have made this garden their home. There are benches and chairs for relaxing, a seven-circuit labyrinth to walk, and a gazebo for enjoying afternoon tea.

"We stayed three nights at this lovely b&b in a great neighborhood… Our hostess, Adele Northrup, was very welcoming. We stayed in a very comfortable bedroom with sofa, TV, and garden views… Snacks and drinks were provided in a little basket in our rooms (fresh bottled water everyday, sweet and savory snacks) and we were told to help ourselves to beer from her fridge if we so wished. Breakfast was different everyday and boy was it plentiful!… Do stay here, it is a wonderful place." —Guest

INNKEEPER: Adele Northrup

ADDRESS: 630 Orme Circle, N.E., Atlanta, Georgia 30306

TELEPHONE: (404) 892-2735

E-MAIL: adele@virginiahighlandbb.com

WEBSITE: www.virginiahighlandbb.com

ROOMS: 3 Rooms; 1 Suite; Private baths

CHILDREN: Welcome; Call ahead

PETS: Not allowed

Banana Coconut Cream

Makes 8-10 Servings

*"I like to have a fruit dip to occupy my guests while
I'm getting food on the table."*

—INNKEEPER, *Virginia Highland Bed & Breakfast*

8 very ripe bananas
1 teaspoon vanilla extract
1 cup botanical medic raw coconut oil
Fresh fruit, to serve

Place the bananas, vanilla, and coconut oil in Vita Mix blender or food processor and combine until smooth.

Serve with fresh strawberries or other fruit of choice.

GARDEN HOUSE B&B

This small bed & breakfast, located in a quiet residential neighborhood in Decatur, Georgia, offers vacationers an authentic home-away-from-home lodging experience. The private second-floor suite includes a large bedroom, sitting room, and private bath. The inn's screened-in porch looks out over the private garden and is the perfect place to relax in the afternoon or early-morning hours.

A hearty Southern-style breakfast is included with each guest's stay and features innkeeper Rhoda's famous cinnamon rolls and muffins. Other breakfast items range from grits, eggs, sausage, and biscuits to blintzes, quiche, and fresh baked bread.

INNKEEPERS: Doug & Rhoda Joyner

ADDRESS: 135 Garden Lane, Decatur, Georgia 30030

TELEPHONE: (404) 377-3057

E-MAIL: reservations@gardenhousebedandbreakfastdecatur.com

WEBSITE: http://gardenhousebedandbreakfastdecatur.com

ROOMS: 1 Suite; Private bath

CHILDREN: Welcome

PETS: Not allowed

Breakfast Fruit Casserole

Makes 12 Servings

"You can use any seasonal fruit in this casserole.
This one has apples and cranberries, but you could use blueberries,
blackberries, peaches, and apples in any combination."
—INNKEEPER, *Garden House Bed & Breakfast*

3 cups deiced unpeeled apples
2 cups whole raw cranberries
1½ cups sugar
1 stick butter, melted

Crunchy Topping:
⅓ cup brown sugar
½ cup flour
¾ teaspoon salt
1⅓ cups quick-cook oats
½ cup chopped pecans

Preheat oven to 350°F. In a medium bowl, mix together fruit and
sugar. Pour mixture into a greased 9x11-inch pan. In a separate
medium bowl, combine topping ingredients and sprinkle over the
top of the fruit. Pour the melted butter over the top of the casserole
and bake 1 hour until topping is browned.

THE INN AT FOLKSTON

The Inn at Folkston is a restored 1920s bungalow located in the quaint town of Folkston, in southeast Georgia. Guests will enjoy the peace and quiet that surrounds them and creates a luxurious and relaxing refuge. Each of the inn's four guest rooms is uniquely decorated and feature deluxe feather beds covered in soft down comforters. Fresh flowers and an eclectic mix of antiques, oriental,

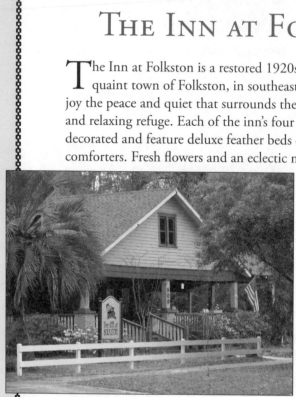

and modern furnishings can be found throughout the inn.

While the inn and its elegant accommodations inspire rest and relaxation, there are still plenty of area activities for the whole family can enjoy. The Okefenokee Wildlife Refuge is just ten minutes from the inn. There, nature enthusiasts can enjoy group boat and motorboat tours, kayaking, canoeing, and even biking. Okenfenokee Sporting Clays is also nearby and boasts tournament grade target shooting. Visitors will also find great train watching, civil war era forts and museums, local wineries, and the Wild Adventures theme park, all just a short drive away.

INNKEEPERS: Janis Richtmeyer & William Whitaker

ADDRESS: 509 West Main Street, Folkston, Georgia 31537

TELEPHONE: (912) 496-6256; (888) 509-6246

E-MAIL: info@innatfolkston.com

WEBSITE: www.innatfolkston.com

ROOMS: 4 Rooms; Private baths

CHILDREN: Welcome

PETS: Not allowed; Resident pets

Ozark

Makes 4-5 Servings

1 egg
¾ cup sugar
2 tablespoons flour
1¼ teaspoon baking powder
1 teaspoon vanilla extract
¼ teaspoon salt
½ cup chopped nuts
1 medium to large apple,
     coarsely chopped

Preheat oven to 350°F. Mix together the egg, sugar, flour, baking powder, vanilla, and salt; add nuts and apples. Pour mixture into 2-quart buttered casserole dishes and bake 20–25 minutes.

The Ozark crust will puff and bubble during baking but will flatten when cooled. Serve warm or cold with whipped cream.

Breakfast Cookies

Makes 2 dozen

1 pound butter
2 cups brown sugar
2 cups white sugar
2 medium eggs
1 egg yolk
2 teaspoons vanilla extract
5 cups all-purpose flour
2 cups oats
2 cups bran
2 teaspoons baking soda
2 teaspoons baking powder
½ teaspoon salt
1 cup walnuts or pecans
1 cup raisins or Craisins
1 cup chocolate chips

Preheat oven to 350°F. In a large bowl, cream together butter and sugars; add eggs and vanilla to mixture. Add flour, oats, bran, baking soda, baking powder, and salt, stirring by hand. Batter should be fairly stiff; if batter is sticky, add small amounts of additional flour as needed. Using hands, add nuts, raisins, and chocolate chips to the batter.

Drop by ¼-cupfuls onto an ungreased cookie sheet. Bake 12–13 minutes, being careful not to overbake.

Poached Pears with Cranberry Cream

Makes 4-6 Servings

Pears:
4-6 firm pears (1 per person)
1/2 cup water
2 tablespoons sugar

Cranberry Sauce:
1 cup fresh or frozen cranberries, ground
1 cup sour cream
$\frac{1}{3}$ cup honey
½ teaspoon orange rind
1 teaspoon orange juice

For the pears: Preheat oven to 400°F. Slice the bottom off of the pear so that it will stand up. Core the pear using a melon baller – be sure to keep both the pear and the stem end intact. Peel the pear leaving about ½-inch of skin around the stem. In a small bowl, mix together the cinnamon, water, and sugar and pour the mixture into a small casserole dish. Stand the pears in the dish and baste with the liquid. Bake about 20 minutes, until pears are done – test with a toothpick and be careful not to overbake. Serve pears warm or cold with cranberry sauce, cream, or whipped cream.

For the cranberry sauce: Using a blender or food processor, grind the cranberries. Mix in sour cream, honey, orange rind, and orange juice. Test mixture for sweetness and add additional honey if you desire. Pour over pears, or use as a fruit dip.

Simmons-Bond Inn B&B

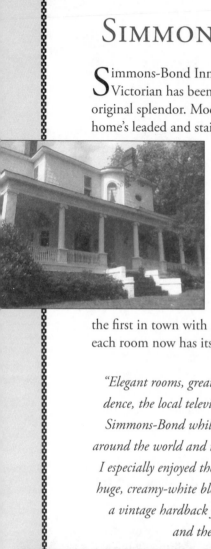

Simmons-Bond Inn, an elegant turn-of-the-century Queen Anne Victorian has been lovingly and painstakingly restored to its original splendor. Modern conveniences combine perfectly with the home's leaded and stained glass windows, oak flooring, pillars and staircase, period antiques and heirlooms, and oriental rugs. Even the original brass chandeliers still hang from the amazing 12-foot ceilings. The inn's 3-course Southern breakfast is served on antique china and crystal and each of the inn's guest rooms feature antique furnishings and décor. Few things have been changed, but merely updated, for example coal fireplaces have been converted to gas and although the home is rumored to have been the first in town with running water, there was only one bathroom; each room now has its own private bath.

"Elegant rooms, great attention to detail, sparkling clean! By coincidence, the local television [station] and newspaper both featured the Simmons-Bond while I was staying there. No surprise. I've traveled around the world and this is one of the most charming b&bs I've found. I especially enjoyed the gracious attention of the young innkeepers, the huge, creamy-white blossoms on the magnolia in the side yard, reading a vintage hardback from the family's library on the wide veranda, and the excellent location…" — Guest

INNKEEPER: Elizabeth Forkey

ADDRESS: 130 West Tugalo Street, Toccoa, Georgia 30577

TELEPHONE: (706) 282-5183; (877) 658-0746

E-MAIL: simmonsbond@juno.com

WEBSITE: www.simmons-bond.com

ROOMS: 5 Rooms; Private baths

CHILDREN: Welcome

PETS: Not allowed

Lemon Poached Pear

Makes 4 Servings

"This delicious and simple recipe was another we featured on the local Cable Access cooking show called Southern Hospitality. Our guests always enjoy this dish." — INNKEEPER, *Simmons-Bond Inn*

2 pears, cut in half lengthwise and cored
1 teaspoon ginger
2 tablespoons lemon juice
Cottage cheese
4 strawberries, cut decoratively
Caramel ice cream topping

Trim a strip of skin off the pear, lengthwise down the middle for presentation. Pour 1½-inches of water into a large skillet or pot; add the ginger and lemon juice and bring to a simmer. Cook the pears in the water for 10 minutes, turning once after 5 minutes. Firmer pears may need longer; softer pears may be done sooner.

Plate each pear half with a spoonful of cottage cheese and a strawberry on the side. Drizzle with caramel sauce and serve.

Pura Vida USA

Pura Vida USA is a unique lodging experience located in lovely Dahlonega, Georgia. This wellness and yoga retreat is committed to providing restful and relaxing vacations designed to help revitalize even the weariest travelers. Set aside your worries and bask in the serene and peaceful setting, over 72 acres of woodland and mountain views, wildflower gardens, and grassland.

While you're there take advantage of the inns wonderful spa treatments and daily yoga classes, attend a tasting at one of the many local wineries, and enjoy the great outdoors. Hike the local nature parks and visit the area waterfalls. Swimming, kayaking, gold mining, and horseback riding are amongst the many other local activities available to guests.

INNKEEPER: Beckie Fairley

ADDRESS: 400 Blueberry Hill, Dahlonega, Georgia 30533

TELEPHONE: (706) 865-7678; (866) 345-4900

E-MAIL: reservations@puravidausa.com

WEBSITE: www.puravidausa.com

ROOMS: 24 Rooms; 1 Suite; 8 Cabins; Private baths

CHILDREN: Welcome

PETS: Small pets welcome

Blueberry Crunch

Makes 9 Servings

"This recipe has been passed down through generations."
—INNKEEPER, *Pura Vida USA*

16 ounces blueberries, fresh or frozen
1 can crushed pineapple, do not drain
½ cup sugar
½ box French vanilla cake mix
½ cup melted butter
1 cup nuts

Preheat oven to 350°F. Spread blueberries over the bottom of a
9x13-inch cake pan. Spread crushed pineapples and juice over
blueberries; sprinkle with sugar. Pour ½ of the boxed cake mix
over the fruit until it is all covered. Spread melted butter over the
cake mix; sprinkle with nuts and bake until brown, 35–45 minutes.

Pura Vida USA Pastry Dough

Makes 1 9x9-inch Shell

This recipe is to be used alongside the Blueberry Pie recipe.
As this is a basic pastry dough recipe, you could also use it for other pies
of your choice. Simply prepare and fill as desired.
Bake in a preheated oven at 375°F for 35–40 minutes.

2 cups flour
1 teaspoon salt
$^2/_3$ cups solid shortening
2 tablespoons ice water
1 teaspoon sugar
1 teaspoon cinnamon

Combine the flour and salt in a large bowl. Cut in the shortening using a pastry cutter or 2 knives until the mixture forms pea-sized pieces. Sprinkle mixture with ice water, 1 tablespoon at a time, tossing with a for until the mixture holds together; press into a ball. Remove dough from bowl and press between your hands to form a disk.

Place dough onto a flat, floured surface. Flour your rolling pin and roll dough to ⅛-inch thickness. Sprinkle dough with additional flour as you roll to prevent sticking. Your dough should be about 1-inch larger than your pie plate.

Blueberry Pie

Makes 1 Pie

2 tablespoons cornstarch
½ cup granulated sugar
¾ cup brown sugar
¼ cup water
1 stick margarine
16 ounces blueberries (frozen or fresh)
1 tablespoon Grand Marnier
2 pie crusts (see previous page)
2 tablespoons butter, melted
Sugar
Cinnamon

Preheat oven to 375°F. Mix together the cornstarch and the sugars and pour into a medium saucepan; add water and butter and cook over low heat until melted. Add the blueberries and cook until the mixture has thickened. Allow mixture to cool and then add the Grand Marnier; set aside and prepare pastry dough according to recipe on page 248.

Place the rolling pin on one side of the pastry dough and roll the dough over the pin to help you place it into your 9x9-inch pie plate. Trim the crust if necessary and pour in blueberry filling. Top the pie with a second complete crust dotted with holes for ventilation or cut into strips for a latticed crust. Brush with butter and sprinkle with sugar and cinnamon. Bake 35-40 minutes until golden brown.

STONEHURST PLACE

Stonehurst Place combines exemplary service with Southern hospitality and charm. You'll feel as though you're staying in a grand hotel, while receiving the personalized attention that only a b&b can provide.

The quaint and cozy Stonehurst Place was originally built in 1896. The home remained with the same family for over a century and, as a result, has retained many of its original turn-of-the-century charms. Owner Barb Shadomy has lovingly restored the home to its original splendor, and added some modern touches that have made the home more eco-friendly and energy efficient. With its lovely gardens and its serene setting, you'll almost forget that you're just a short walk away from Atlanta's theater, museum, and arts district!

INNKEEPER: Rose Marie Ray

ADDRESS: 923 Piedmont Avenue, NE, Atlanta, Georgia 30309

TELEPHONE: (404) 881-0722

E-MAIL: info@stonehurstplace.com

WEBSITE: www.stonehurstplace.com

ROOMS: 1 Room; 1 Suite

CHILDREN: Welcome; Call ahead

PETS: Small dogs welcome; Call ahead

Apple Cake

Makes 9-12 Servings

1 cup oil
1¾ cups sugar
3 eggs
1 teaspoon vanilla extract
1 teaspoon salt
1 teaspoon baking soda
1 teaspoon cinnamon
2 cups flour
4 cups sliced apples or
    1 can Comstock Apple Slices

Preheat oven to 375°F. In a large bowl, combine oil, sugar, eggs, and vanilla. In a separate bowl, sift together salt, baking soda, cinnamon, and flour. Add dry ingredients to wet mixture and mix well to combine. Fold in apple slices. Pour batter into a 9x13-inch pan and bake for 45-60 minutes. You will need to check progress after about 30 minutes as ovens vary.

Serve cake warm with whipped cream or ice cream.

Barn Inn at Lake Rabun

This quiet mountain getaway is truly a unique lodging experience. The inn was indeed once a horse barn that has since been renovated and transformed into a cozy and relaxing vacation retreat. In keeping with inn's original history, each of the guest rooms is named for one of the racing industry's most well-known Triple Crown winners, including Seabiscuit and Man O' War.

Nearby attractions in Lake Rabun include the Tallulah Gorge State Park, hiking trails, horseback riding, kayaking, an even a classic drive-in theater. Whether you choose to remain at the inn and bask in the quiet solitude and gorgeous surroundings, or head into town and enjoy some of the local shopping and dining, Barn Inn at Lake Rabun is a perfect place to relax and get away from it all.

INNKEEPERS: Jan Timms & Nancy Gribble

ADDRESS: 31 Barn Inn Road, Lakemont, Georgia 30552

TELEPHONE: (706) 212-9995

E-MAIL: barninnjan@windstream.net

WEBSITE: www.barninn.com

ROOMS: 6 Rooms; Private baths

CHILDREN: Children ages 14 and older welcome

PETS: Not allowed

Apricot Nectar Cake

Makes 1 Cake

"This recipe was passed along to me by my mother-in-law."

—INNKEEPER, *Barn Inn at Lake Rabun*

1 box yellow cake mix
1 (3 ounce) package lemon Jell-O
¾ cup vegetable oil
4 eggs
3/4 cup apricot nectar
2 tablespoons lemon extract

Icing:
1½ cups powdered sugar
Juice from 2 lemons

Preheat oven to 350°F. In a large bowl, combine yellow cake mix, lemon Jell-O, vegetable oil, eggs, apricot nectar, and lemon extract. Mix until well combined and pour into a well greased and floured bundt pan. Bake for 1 hour. Remove from oven and allow to cool just a few minutes. While the cake is still warm, poke small holes in the top of the cake and pour the icing over.

For the icing: In a small bowl, mix together the sugar and lemon juice.

1890 King-Keith House

L ocated in a National Historic Register of Historic Places neighborhood, just minutes from downtown Atlanta, is a jewel of a bed & breakfast. The 1890 King-Keith House B&B is an elegant and stately Queen Anne Victorian that is beautifully and comfortably furnished. The Southern ambiance and noteworthy hospitality make the King-Keith House one of the most warm and inviting historic bed and breakfasts in all of Atlanta.

"...The bed and breakfast is filled with antiques and yet is still so inviting. Our room was incredible and the breakfast was to die for! We would stay there every night of the year if we could eat that breakfast! The hosts, Jan and Windell, told us everywhere we needed to go to make our visit special...You can't beat the location: right in the heart of downtown and a short walk to the subway station...If you're looking for a unique place to stay and a chance to meet some truly interesting people, we would suggest you stay at the King-Keith House on your next visit to Atlanta..." —Guest

INNKEEPERS: Windell & Janet Keith

ADDRESS: 889 Edgewood Avenue, NE, Atlanta, Georgia 30307

TELEPHONE: (404) 688-7330; (800) 728-3879

E-MAIL: kingkeith@mindspring.com

WEBSITE: www.kingkeith.com

ROOMS: 5 Rooms; 1 Suite; 1 Cottage; Private & shared baths

CHILDREN: Welcome

PETS: Not allowed

World's Best Carrot Cake

Makes 16 Servings

"A legendary favorite with all of the family that's reserved for special occasions. I have also adapted this cake to make mini-muffins for large parties." —INNKEEPER, *1890 King-Keith House*

1½ cups whole wheat flour
⅔ cup all-purpose flour
2 teaspoons baking soda
2 teaspoons cinnamon
½ teaspoon salt
½ teaspoon ground nutmeg
¼ teaspoon ground ginger
1 cup sugar
1 cup brown sugar, firmly packed
1 cup buttermilk
¾ cup vegetable oil
4 eggs
1½ teaspoons vanilla
1 (1-pound) bag carrots,
    peeled and grated

1 (8-ounce) can crushed pineapple,
    drained
1 cup pecans or walnuts, chopped
1 cup flaked coconut
½ cup raisins or currants

Cream Cheese Frosting:
½ cup butter, room temperature
1 (8-ounce) package cream cheese,
    room temperature
1 (16-ounce) package
    confectioners' sugar
2 teaspoons grated orange peel
1 teaspoon vanilla

Preheat oven to 350°F. Sift together the flours, baking soda, cinnamon, salt, nutmeg, and ginger onto a sheet of wax paper. In a large bowl, mix the sugars together; stir in the buttermilk, vegetable oil, eggs, and vanilla. Pour in the flour mixture, carrots, pineapple, nuts, coconut, and raisins or currants, stirring until well blended. Grease and flour 3 9-inch round cake pans. Line the bottoms with wax paper; grease and flour the wax paper. Divide the batter evenly between the three pans and bake 30 minutes, or until a toothpick inserted in the center comes away clean. Cool the cake in the pans for 10 minutes before inverting onto wire racks. Peel off the wax paper and allow layers to cool completely.

For the frosting: Beat the butter and cream cheese together in a large mixing bowl until light. Add the sugar, orange peel, and vanilla and mix well. Spread the frosting between the layers and over the tops and sides of the cake. Cover and refrigerate overnight before cutting.

LUCILLE'S
MOUNTAIN TOP INN

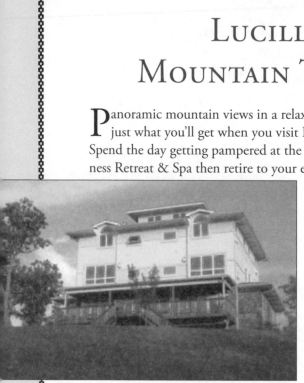

Panoramic mountain views in a relaxing and romantic setting are just what you'll get when you visit Lucille's Mountain Top Inn. Spend the day getting pampered at the attached Mandala Wellness Retreat & Spa then retire to your elegant and cozy room. The following day, wake to a gourmet breakfast and set off for shopping in nearby Helen. Hike the national forest, explore the state park waterfalls, mine for gold, or go hot air ballooning. Whatever you choose, luxury accommodations await you each evening at Lucille's Mountain Top Inn.

"… The rooms are lovely, with large windows to enjoy the breathtaking view. We would get up very early to watch the deer come up to the inn for breakfast. And speaking of breakfast! Every morning was a delight. We had breakfast casseroles, French toast, and too many other good things to note…" —GUEST

INNKEEPERS: Lucille Hlavenka

ADDRESS: 964 Rabun Road, Sautee, Georgia 30571

TELEPHONE: (706) 878-5055; (866) 245-4777

E-MAIL: stay@lucillesmountaintopinn.com

WEBSITE: www.lucillesmountaintopinn.com

ROOMS: 9 Rooms; Private baths

CHILDREN: Children age 14 and older welcome

PETS: Not allowed; Resident pets

Ice Box Fruit Cake

Makes 24 Servings

"People who don't like fruitcake love mine!"

—INNKEEPER, *Lucille's Mountain Top Inn*

1 pound dates
1½ cups pecans
1½ cups walnuts
1 pound candied cherries (half red, half green)
3 cups graham cracker crumbs
1 large package coconut
2 (14-ounce) cans Eagle brand
   Sweetened Condensed Milk

Chop the dates, cherries, and nuts; mix with graham cracker crumbs. Add the coconut flakes and sweetened condensed milk and blend thoroughly. Press wax paper into two large (10-inch) bread pans and fill with fruitcake mixture, pressing down hard to fill spaces.

Cake must be refrigerated when not serving and can also be frozen.

Pennsylvania Dutch Cake & Custard Pie

Makes 1 Pie

"This recipe is adapted from the Pillsbury Best of the Bake-Off Cookbook.*"* —INNKEEPER, *Lucille's Mountain Top Inn*

1 (15-ounce) refrigerated pie crust

Filling:
⅓ cup sugar
2 tablespoons flour
1 teaspoon apple pie spice
1 cup applesauce
⅔ cup sour cream
⅓ cup molasses
1 egg, beaten

Glaze:
½ cup confectioner's sugar
2 tablespoons coffee

Cake:
½ cup sugar
¼ cup butter
½ cup buttermilk
1 egg
1 teaspoon vanilla
1¼ cups flour
1 teaspoon baking powder
¼ teaspoon salt
¼ teaspoon baking soda

Preheat oven to 350°F. Prepare the pie crust according to package directions for one crust filled pie using a 9-inch pie plate. In a medium bowl, mix together filling ingredients combining dry ingredients first and then stirring in remaining filling ingredients. Set aside.

For the cake: In a small bowl, combine sugar and butter and beat until well blended. Beat in buttermilk, egg, and vanilla. Add remaining cake ingredients and mix well. Spoon into pie crust and carefully top with filling mixture. Bake 50-65 minutes, or until the center of the cake springs back when touched lightly and top is golden brown. In a small bowl, combine sugar and coffee until it is your desired consistency. Drizzle over warm pie and serve.

Hot Fudge Pudding Cake

Makes 6-8 Small Servings

"Nearly all of my luncheons request this for dessert every time!"

—INNKEEPER, *Lucille's Mountain Top Inn*

Bottom Layer:
1 cup brown sugar, packed
1 cup flour
3 tablespoons cocoa powder
2 teaspoons baking powder
¼ teaspoon salt
½ cup milk
2 tablespoons butter, melted
½ teaspoon chocolate extract

Top Layer:
¾ cup brown sugar, packed
¼ cup cocoa powder
1¾ cup boiling water
Nuts, whipped cream, ice cream,
and cherries to serve

For the bottom layer: In a large bowl, mix together brown sugar, flour, cocoa, baking powder, and salt. Stir in milk, butter, and chocolate extract. Place a crock pot liner in a large crock pot and spread in the batter for the bottom layer of the cake.

For the top layer: In a small bowl, combine the brown sugar and cocoa and sprinkle over the batter for the bottom layer. Pour in boiling water. Do not stir. Cover the crock pot and cook on high for 2-3 hours, or until a knife inserted in the center comes away clean. Serve warm with any topping you like.

LAFAYETTE MANOR INN

In addition to earning the AAA 3-Diamond award for accommodations, the Lafayette Manor Inn has also been awarded the AAA 3-Diamond award for its fine cuisine. Owners Guillaume and Sokunvathany are passionate chefs, who spend hours in search of the freshest ingredients from local farmers' markets and or-

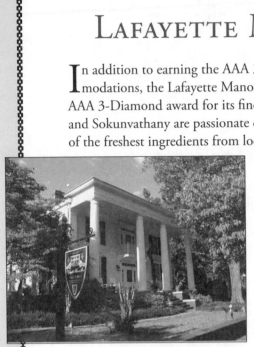

ganic farms. For lunch, they serve French Bistro-style fare in their casual dining room or outside on the porch. Menu items include their smoked salmon salad, lobster and crab ravioli, and a daily soup.

For dinner, the inn has a five-course meal served in the formal dining room that ends with a private piano concerto. Although dinner items change daily, past entrées include free-range chicken breast with leeks, sautéed veal with citrus sauce, New York strip in a champagne sauce, and sea bass with fennel sauce. Appetizers, soup, salad, and dessert are also included. In addition to serving these succulent items, the inn also offers an all-inclusive cooking class package and will teach you to recreate menu items on your own.

INNKEEPERS: Guillaume & Sokunvathany Slama

ADDRESS: 219 East Robert Toombs Avenue, Washington, Georgia 30673

TELEPHONE: (706) 678-5922

E-MAIL: info@lafayettemanor.com

WEBSITE: http://lafayettemanor.com

ROOMS: 7 Rooms; 1 Suite; 1 Cottage; Private baths

CHILDREN: Children age 8 and older welcome

PETS: Dogs allowed; Resident pets

Fondant au Chocolat

Makes 4 Servings

*"We call this Melting Chocolate Cake. Our guests wanted
to change the name of this dessert to 'Chocolate Decadence.'
We like to keep its name the way it is because we watch our
guests 'melt' while they eat it!"* —INNKEEPER, *Lafayette Manor*

3½ ounces Nestlé's
   semi-sweet morsels
8 pieces of Nestlé's Baker
   semi-sweet chocolate
3 eggs
2¾ ounces sugar
1¾ ounces butter
1 tablespoon flour

Butter the bottom of 4 ramekins and preheat oven to 500°F.
Melt the chocolate morsels in a glass bowl over a water bath and
add the butter. In a separate bowl, mix together the eggs, sugar,
and flour. Add the melted chocolate mixture and mix thoroughly.
Pour the mixture into the ramekins until they are half-filled. Add
2 pieces of the semi-sweet chocolate to the center of each ramekin
and then top with the rest of the mixture. Bake about 10 minutes
and serve lukewarm.

The Gastonian

Located in the heart of Savannah's historic district, and made up of two nineteenth century mansions, the Gastonian is one of Savannah's most elegant and luxurious inns. The service is warm and friendly, and the accommodations are nothing short of spectacular. Complimentary wine and hors d'oeuvres are served each afternoon and dessert and cordials are served each evening. The

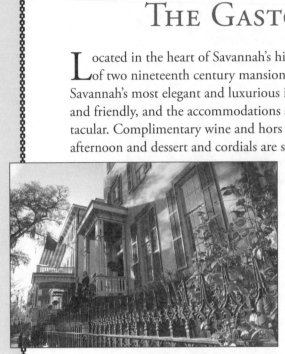

inn's warm and friendly staff will gladly help guests with restaurant reservations, tickets to shows, and recommendations for other area attractions. When you return in the evening you'll find your bed turned down and pralines waiting on your pillow.

Each of the inn's rooms is outfitted with deluxe linens and luxury bath products, claw-foot or whirlpool tubs, and antique furniture. A gourmet breakfast is included with your stay and can be served family-style in the inn's elegant dining room, or in your guest suite.

INNKEEPER:	Melanie Bliss
ADDRESS:	220 East Gaston Street, Savannah, Georgia 31401
TELEPHONE:	(912) 232-2869; (800) 322-6603
E-MAIL:	concierge@gastonian.com
WEBSITE:	www.gastonian.com
ROOMS:	15 Rooms; 2 Suites; Private baths
CHILDREN:	Children age 12 and older welcome
PETS:	Not allowed

Almond Skillet Cake

Makes 1 Cake

"This dessert is a simple recipe that is loved by our guests. Plan ahead, you will need to bake this the day before you plan on serving it." —INNKEEPER, *The Gastonian*

¾ cup butter or margarine, melted
1½ cups sugar
2 eggs
1½ cups sifted all-purpose flour
Pinch of salt
1 teaspoon almond flavor
Sliced almonds
Extra sugar

Preheat oven to 350°F. In a large mixing bowl, combine the melted butter and the sugar; mix well. Beat in the eggs, one at a time. Add the flour, salt, and almond flavoring and mix well. Line an iron skillet with aluminum foil, letting the foil hang over the sides. Put the batter in the skillet, cover with the almonds and sprinkle with additional sugar. Bake 40 minutes. Allow cake to fully cool before removing from the skillet. Do not slice until the following day.

ROTHSCHILD POUND HOUSE

B uilt in the 1870s, this elegant and historic Victorian home was almost lost to neglect. The home was saved thanks to community effort and was lovingly restored in 1994. The inn now boasts 16 stately appointed guest rooms spread throughout the main house and the ground's six cottages. Luxury bath products and robes can be found in each of the rooms, and if you choose, you can have champagne and chocolates for two set up for a romantic evening.

Evening cocktails and hors d'oeuvres as well as a hearty Southern breakfast are all part of your stay. You can choose to eat en-suite or in the dining room. Each of the rooms has its own mini-fridge and coffee maker; cottages also feature their own wet bar/kitchen and parlor.

INNKEEPER: Kristen Jocums

ADDRESS: 201 7th Street, Columbus, Georgia 31901

TELEPHONE: (706) 322-4075

E-MAIL: info@thepoundhouseinn.com

WEBSITE: www.thepoundhouseinn.com

ROOMS: 8 Rooms; 4 Suites; 6 Cottages; Private baths

CHILDREN: Welcome

PETS: Welcome

Pecan Praline Cheesecake

Makes 1 Cake

¾ cup graham cracker crumbs
½ cup pecans, toasted and chopped
⅓ cup brown sugar
¼ cup melted butter
½ cup heath bar chips
3 (8-ounce) packages cream cheese, softened
1 (14-ounce) can sweetened condensed milk
3 eggs
2 teaspoons vanilla extract

Topping:
⅓ cup brown sugar
⅓ cup whipping cream
⅓ cup toasted and chopped pecans

Preheat oven to 300°F. In a small bowl, mix together crumbs, pecans, brown sugar, and butter. Press the mixture into the bottom of a 9-inch springform pan and bake 8-10 minutes. Remove from oven and spread the heath bar chips over the crust. In a small bowl, mix together the cream cheese, sweetened condensed milk, eggs, and vanilla until very smooth. Pour the batter over the heath chips and bake 50-60 minutes, until the center is set.

Allow to cool 10 minutes then sprinkle additional heath bar chips over the top of the cheesecake.

For the topping: In a small saucepan, heat the sugar with the whipping cream until the sugar has dissolved. Remove from heat, add the nuts and smooth over the top of the cake.

NORTH AVENUE CARRIAGE HOUSE

Narth Avenue Carriage House is conveniently located just a short walk from the Ellijay town square. You can visit Corks and Crumbs, the town's wine tasting room and bakery, do some antique shopping, and visit the town museum, all by foot. Just a short drive away, you'll find Amicalola Falls and Fort Mountain state parks, both of which are great hiking and picnic spots. Nearby Carters Lake is a great place for boating and fishing. Other area activities include golf, tennis, and bicycling.

Between the months of May and November, Ellijay, Georgia is host to a wide variety of festivals and special events including the Taste of Ellijay, Ellijay Under the Stars, and the Apple Festival.

INNKEEPERS:	Les & Ouida Leech
ADDRESS:	41 North Avenue, Ellijay, Georgia 30540
TELEPHONE:	(706) 889-5658
E-MAIL:	oleech@gmail.com
WEBSITE:	www.northavenuecarriagehouse.com
ROOMS:	3 Rooms; 2 Suites; 1 Cottage; Private baths
CHILDREN:	Children age 6 and older welcome
PETS:	Not allowed

French Coconut Pie

Makes 6-8 Servings

½ stick butter
1 tablespoon flour
1 cup fresh, shredded coconut
1 teaspoon vanilla extract
½ cup egg beaters
¾ cup sugar
1 cup milk
1 9-inch unbaked pie crust

Preheat oven to 400°F. Melt the butter and pour into a medium bowl. Mix in flour, coconut, vanilla, egg beaters, sugar, and milk. Once all ingredients are fully incorporated, pour the mixture into the pie crust and bake 45-60 minutes, until pie is firm.

Cream pies are amongst the most popular pies in America today. People who are passionate about their cream pies often prefer the many varieties to traditional fruit pies. Because these pies are less dependent on seasonal ingredients, they are great for making year-round.

THE WHITLOCK INN

The Whitlock Inn, also known as the "Jewel of Marietta," is a grand old Victorian located in a National Historic Register district, just one block from historic Marietta Town Square. Built in 1900, the inn has been fully renovated and now features five separate guest rooms. The inn also has a large ballroom that can accommodate over 100 people, smaller rooms available for intimate luncheons and meetings, and a lush garden that's perfect for out-

door parties. Whether you're planning a small get-together for family and friends, a weekend getaway for you and your sweetheart, or even an elegant Southern wedding, Whitlock is the place for you.

Each guest at the Whitlock Inn will enjoy a hearty continental breakfast with selections such as homemade quiche, breads, muffins, fresh fruit, juice, and tea to get them going. Just a short walk brings you to the heart of historic Marietta where you'll find excellent antique shops, golf at the Marietta City Club, tennis at Laurel Park, beautiful sightseeing, and a host of delicious restaurants. Kennesaw Mountain National Battlefield is great for history buffs looking to learn more about the Civil War era – there are even reenactment battles during the summer. After a busy afternoon, you can relax and enjoy a carriage ride around the square and return to the inn for a restful evening.

INNKEEPER: Alexis Amaden

ADDRESS: 57 Whitlock Avenue, Marietta, Georgia 30064

TELEPHONE: (770) 428-1495

E-MAIL: whitlockinn@hotmail.com

WEBSITE: www.whitlockinn.com

ROOMS: 5 rooms; Private baths

CHILDREN: Children age 12 and older welcome

PETS: Not allowed

Edward's Pecan Pie

Makes 1 Pie

1 9-inch unbaked pie crust
1 cup light corn syrup
1 cup firmly packed brown sugar
3 eggs, slightly beaten
1/3 cup butter, melted
1/2 teaspoon salt
1 teaspoon vanilla
1 heaping cup halved pecans

Preheat oven to 350°F. In a large bowl, combine all ingredients except pecans; mix well. Pour mixture into the pie shell and sprinkle with pecans. Bake 45-50 minutes, until center is set and a toothpick inserted in the center comes away clean.

Candied Spiced Pecans

Makes 1 Batch

1 cup water
1 cup sugar
2 cups halved pecans
1 dash cayenne pepper
1 additional cup of sugar

Boil water and 1 cup of sugar together until golden; add pecans and cook for 1 minute. Strain pecans with a metal strainer and place in the additional cup of loose sugar; stir. Allow the pecans to cool and then pull them from the sugar and place on a drying rack. If desired, sprinkle with cayenne pepper.

After the pecans dry, they can be stored in a Ziploc bag for up to 3 months.

Kesha's Oatmeal Butterscotch Cookies

Makes 2–3 Dozen, depending on size

⅔ cup sugar
⅔ cup packed brown sugar
½ cup margarine or butter, softened
½ cup shortening
1 teaspoon baking soda
1 teaspoon ground cinnamon
1 teaspoon vanilla extract
½ teaspoon baking powder
½ teaspoon salt
2 large eggs
3 cups quick-cooking or old-fashioned oats
1 cup all-purpose flour
1½ cups butterscotch chips

Preheat oven to 375°F. In a large bowl, combine sugar, brown sugar, butter, shortening, baking soda, cinnamon, vanilla, baking powder, salt, and eggs. Mix well. Gradually stir in oats, flour, and butterscotch chips. Drop dough by rounded teaspoonfuls onto a greased cookie sheet; space cookies about 2 inches apart. Bake 9-11 minutes, or until light brown.

JEKYLL ISLAND CLUB HOTEL

The elegant Jekyll Island Club Hotel is a self-supporting luxury resort located on beautiful Jekyll Island. The resort compound has 157 guest rooms and suites, in five different historical settings. You can choose to stay in the Clubhouse, or main hotel, Annex, San Souci, or one of the two elegant cottages. The Crane Cottage, built in 1917 in the classic Italianate style has 13 guest rooms, lush gardens, and courtyard dining. The Cherokee Cottage, built in 1904, has 10 guest rooms. There are a total of four restaurants in the compound. The Grand Dining room serves breakfast, lunch, dinner, and the famous Sunday Brunch. Café Solterra is the inn's bakery and delicatessen and offers lighter fare. The courtyard at Crane serves California wine-country cuisine. There is also a poolside bar and grill.

The gorgeous grounds offer a wide array of activities for guests including golf, charter fishing, and, of course, swimming. With over ten miles of white sand beaches, Jekyll Island is a mecca for sun-bathers and water lovers. Shelling, swimming, sunning, and horse-back riding are just a few of the beachfront activities available.

INNKEEPER: Kevin Runner
ADDRESS: 371 Riverview Drive, Jekyll Island, Georgia 31527
TELEPHONE: (912) 635-2600; (800) 535-9547
E-MAIL: mail@jekyllclub.com
WEBSITE: www.jekyllclub.com
ROOMS: 122 Rooms; 35 Suites: 5 Cottages; Private baths
CHILDREN: Welcome
PETS: Not allowed

Millionaire Blueberry Bars

Makes 1 9x11x2-Inch Pan

*"These blueberry dessert bars are best when fresh berries are used –
the way Jekyll's millionaires preferred them. The almond extract
and cream cheese are the perfect ingredients to give the dessert
just the right taste with a hint of Southern flavor."*

—INNKEEPER, *Jekyll Island Club Hotel*

Crust:
½ pound butter
½ cup sugar
1 cup plus 2 tablespoons
   bread flour
Pinch of cinnamon

Filling:
5 whole eggs
1¾ cups brown sugar
1½ teaspoons vanilla
¾ teaspoon salt

1½ cups fresh or
   frozen blueberries
Flour to coat
1 cup crushed walnuts
Pinch of cinnamon

Icing:
1 pound cream cheese
¾ cup powdered sugar
1 teaspoon vanilla
½ teaspoon almond extract

For the crust: Preheat oven to 325°F. Cream the butter and sugar
until smooth; add the flour and cinnamon and mix until combined.
Press dough into the bottom of a buttered 9x11x2-inch pan. Bake
until light brown, or half-baked, approximately 8-10 minutes.
Remove and let cool.

For the filling: Whisk eggs and brown sugar in a bowl until smooth;
stir in vanilla and salt. Toss the blueberries in flour, shaking off
any excess. Fold walnuts and blueberries into sugar mixture;
add cinnamon. Pour into pre-baked crust and bake until firm,
approximately 30 minutes remove and chill overnight. Ice the
bars the next day and cut into squares.

For the icing: Cream powdered sugar and cheese until smooth;
add vanilla and almond extract and drizzle over bars.

Traveler's Rest B&B

Step back in time, into a charming escape from a hectic, hurry-up world. Here the pace is easy – as active or relaxed as you choose. The accommodations are romantic and timeless, the service friendly and attentive. Regardless of the occasion – vacation, honeymoon, anniversary, or getaway weekend – Traveler's Rest will provide you with a most enjoyable experience.

"If you're looking for a little getaway, this is the place – great value for your money, Adele, the innkeeper, is attentive without being overbearing, and it's even pet- friendly. We just curled up and watched movies from Adele's selection and took some time to visit Andersonville and Plains." — GUEST

INNKEEPER: Adele Goodman

ADDRESS: 318 North Dooly Street, Montezuma, Georgia 31063

TELEPHONE: (478) 472-0085

E-MAIL: info@travelersrestbb.com

WEBSITE: www.travelersrestbb.com

ROOMS: 1 Room; 2 Suites; 1 Carriage House; Private baths

CHILDREN: Welcome; Call ahead

PETS: Welcome

Meringues

Makes 6 Servings

"Delight your guests with this tea-time delight!"

—INNKEEPER, *Traveler's Rest B&B*

3 egg whites
1 cup sugar
1 teaspoon vanilla essence
1 teaspoon water
1 teaspoon vinegar
Strawberries, or fruit of choice, for garnish
Whipped cream, for garnish

Preheat oven to 220°F. Line a cookie sheet with wax paper. In a medium bowl, beat egg whites until they are stiff, gradually adding sugar. Add the vanilla, water, and vinegar.

Drop tablespoon-size spoonfuls of the mixture onto the cookie sheet. Bake 10 minutes, reduce oven temp to 200°F and bake 2 hours. Serve with strawberries and cream.

These can be stored up to 1 month in a sealed container.

Southern Traditions

Southern Traditions

Southerners are passionate about their food;
it's a common bond that brings together families
and communities. Recipes are passed down
through generations of family members, given
to newlyweds as gifts, and shared with strangers
who are entranced by the cuisine, with each
person adding their own influences and special
touches to the dish. Here you will find recipes
for some of Georgia's favorite dishes.

The 1842 Inn's Mint Julep

Makes 1 Mint Julep

*This sweet Southern favorite is traditionally served
in a pewter or silver cup. To drink, hold the cup by the bottom
so that a frost is allowed to form on the glass.*

Mint Syrup:
Handful fresh mint
Water
Sugar

1 Silver mint julep cup
Crushed ice
1 ounce Southern Comfort or
    bourbon of choice
½ ounce Amber Bacardi rum
Angostura aromatic bitters

For the mint syrup: Boil the mint until the water turns green; strain into a glass pitcher. Add one cup of sugar for each quart of hot water and mix until sugar is dissolved. This syrup can be stored in the refrigerator for 3 days.

Fill one mint julep cup with ice; add bourbon and rum. Stir in enough mint syrup to fill the cup and add 2 drops of bitters. Garnish with lemon and fresh mint.

Ashford Manor Mint Julep

Makes 1 Mint Julep

"Leave it to these transplanted Yankees in Watkinsville to mess with a Southern icon. The 'classic' version of this recipe calls for a shot of bitters, we substitute Italian Campari. It enhances the color of the liquid as it mingles with the ice and mint. And, Campari's complexity of bitter flavors provides this Southern staple with a Continental sophistication." —INNKEEPER, *Ashford Manor*

1 shot bourbon
¼ shot Campari
3 shots simple syrup*
Fresh mint sprigs
1 silver mint julep cup

In a small pitcher, stir together bourbon, Campari, simple syrup, and mint sprigs. Pour over crushed ice and serve in a silver mint julep cup. Garnish with mint sprig and powdered sugar.

We recommend enjoying this drink while sitting in a rocker on your favorite porch!

*For simple syrup: Mix together 1 part water with 1 part sugar and boil until sugar has dissolved. Chill.

Citrus Iced Tea

Makes 2 Quarts

Sweet tea is a Southern staple. The sugar is added while the tea is still hot so that each glass is perfectly sweetened and no one has to wait for the sugar to melt! This citrusy version of the Southern favorite comes courtesy of the Olde Savannah Inn.

4 family sized tea bags, black tea
8 cups water (2 cups per family sized bag)
2 cups sugar
1 cup pineapple juice
1 cup orange juice
4 tablespoons lemon juice
Strawberry slices
Lemon slices

Boil tea bags in water for 10 minutes. Remove from heat and squeeze excess water from bags. Stir sugar into hot tea until it is fully dissolved. Add pineapple juice, orange juice, and lemon juice.

Serve tea with crushed ice and garnish with strawberry and lemon slices.

Partridge Inn
Fried Green Tomatoes

Makes 6 Servings

The Partridge Inn has put a new spin on a classic Southern dish.
They serve their Fried Green Tomatoes with a spinach salad and top
the whole thing off with a sweet balsamic syrup.

2 tablespoons hot sauce
1 quart buttermilk
2 pounds cornmeal
3 whole green tomatoes,
    sliced ¼-inch thick
½ cup vegetable oil
12 ounces spinach
4 ounces candied pecans
6 ounces goat cheese
4 ounces balsamic vinegar
3 tablespoons balsamic syrup

In a medium bowl, mix together hot sauce and buttermilk; season with fresh cracked black pepper. Place the cornmeal in a large shallow dish. Dredge the tomato slices in the buttermilk and allow excess to drip off, then coat with cornmeal. Reserve on a sheet pan lined with parchment paper. Heat vegetable oil in a large cast-iron skillet over medium heat. Pan fry the tomatoes until golden-brown and crispy on both sides (3-4 minutes per side). Carefully remove the tomatoes and drain on paper towels.

To serve: In a large bowl, toss the spinach, candied pecans, goat cheese, and balsamic vinegar with a pinch of salt and pepper (to taste). Place three fried tomato slices on each plate and top with the salad, drizzle balsamic syrup over the plate.

Open Gates B&B Shrimp & Grits

Makes 4 Servings

This famous Southern dish is perfect
for breakfast, lunch, and dinner!

Grits
25 large fresh shrimp
1 lemon
2 tablespoons olive oil
1 sweet onion, chopped
1 green bell pepper, chopped
1 red bell pepper, chopped
Salt and pepper, to taste
1 sprig fresh rosemary, finely chopped
2 tablespoons all-purpose flour
1 (12-ounce) can chicken broth

Prepare four servings of grits per package directions. Peel and devein shrimp; marinate in a bowl with the juice of one lemon.* Heat the olive oil in a deep skillet; add the chopped onion and peppers. Season with salt, pepper, and rosemary, and sauté 3 minutes. Sprinkle in the flour and stir to mix. Add the chicken broth and heat until the mixture thickens. Add the shrimp just before you are ready to serve and cook until the shrimp are pink. Ladle gravy and shrimp over the grits and serve immediately.

*The shrimp can be marinated the night before simply store in an air-tight container in the refrigerator.

Dump O Peach

Makes 6 Servings

Dump cake is truly a Southern tradition. Just about every family has their own recipe for this quick and easy dessert. This particular version features a layer of sweet Georgia peaches and comes courtesy of Lucille's Mountain Top Inn.

2 cups fresh peach slices
1 tablespoon cornstarch
½ teaspoon vanilla extract
¼ cup brown sugar
½ teaspoon cinnamon
1 (9-ounce) Jiffy brand white cake mix
   or ½ package 2 layer sized cake mix
4 tablespoons melted butter

Line a crock pot with a Reynolds liner. In a small bowl, toss together the peach slices with the cornstarch; layer over the bottom of the liner. Drizzle vanilla over the peaches and sprinkle with brown sugar and cinnamon. Top with the cake mix. Drizzle the melted butter evenly over the cake mix. Cover the crock pot and cook on high for 3–3½ hours.

Geographical Index of B&Bs

Alphabetical Index of B&Bs

Recipe Index

The Bed & Breakfast Cookbook Series

New England Bed & Breakfast Cookbook
(CT, MA, ME, NH, RI, & VT)
$19.95 / 320 pages / ISBN 978-1-889593-12-8

North Carolina Bed & Breakfast Cookbook
$19.95 / 320 pages / ISBN 978-1-889593-08-1

Pennsylvania Bed & Breakfast Cookbook
$19.95 / 304 pages / ISBN 978-1-889593-18-0

Virginia Bed & Breakfast Cookbook
$19.95 / 320 pages / ISBN 978-1-889593-14-2

Washington State Bed & Breakfast Cookbook
$19.95 / 320 pages / ISBN 978-1-889593-05-0

Texas Bed & Breakfast Cookbook revised and updated
$19.95 / 304 pages / ISBN 978-1-889593-20-3

California Bed & Breakfast revised and updated
$19.95 / 312 pages / ISBN 978-1-889593-21-0

Georgia Bed & Breakfast Cookbook
$21.95 / 296 pages / ISBN 978-1-889593-19-7

Coming this Fall

Florida Bed and Breakfast Cookbook
$21.95 / 296 pages / ISBN 978-1-889593-22-7

Also Available from 3D Press

Southern Church Suppers
$19.95 / 306 pages / ISBN 978-1-889593-16-6

High Altitude Baking
$14.95 / 192 pages / ISBN 978-1-889593-15-9

3D Press, a division of Big Earth Publishing
3005 Center Green Drive • Suite 220 • Boulder, CO 80301

TO ORDER, CALL: (800) 258-5830 or (303) 541-1506 or Fax: (303) 443-9687
or visit our website at www.bigearthpublishing.com